*As always, I want to thank God for
His call on my life and His lavished grace.
One of the greatest expressions
of that grace is the gift
of my wife and life partner, Cindy.*

Sola deo Gloria!

INTRODUCTION

I have told my story so many times when speaking around the world on Business as Mission that it almost seems redundant to do so here. However, because my journey informs my understanding of Scripture (as well as the other way around) and particularly business as mission I think it is helpful as a context for what we will discuss together in this book.

God graciously invaded my life in early 1974. Actually He had been battering at the gate of my self-centered fortress for some time prior but it was in February of that year that, like Lydia, the Lord opened my heart and I believed. My conversion was dramatic. Not emotional. No fireworks. Yet one man knelt down to meet Christ and another, entirely new person got up to live for Him. Within a week I had connected with 3 other new believers on the campus of the University of Tennessee. We all faced a common dilemma. What do Christians do on Friday night? We were expert in what pagans do. But what about the followers of Jesus? Not knowing any better we decided to get together to read the Bible, to pray together and to play cards. That first evening there were 4 of us. The next week there were 8. Then 16 and so on until soon over 150 students and young people began to gather to study the Word, to pray, and eventually to exercise baptism, the Lord's Supper and Church Discipline. Without our knowing it God had used us to plant a New Testament church. I, along with a couple of others became the "elders" and "pastors" of this congregation and from that point I spent the next 15 years in a pastoral role for several different churches around the U.S. I jokingly refer to myself as the "accidental church planter" because only God could have engineered such a path.

I went on to study at a variety of institutions--missionary training schools, Bible colleges, non-Christian universities, earned a BA and eventually gained a Th.M. from one of the finest seminaries in the world. God was gracious and my ministry was effective and blessed. Two churches were planted and two others equipped to serve Christ in their community and in global missions. It was a good season and I thoroughly enjoyed it.

However, over the course of the 15 years that I was in the formal pastorate the Lord began to create in my heart a thirst to be more effective in reaching unbelievers and encouraging believers who were distant from the organized church. I began to sense that my "pastoral job" was actually more of a barrier to this desire rather than a bridge. Let me quickly say that this was for me and not for all those engaged in pastoral work.

Over time, the Holy Spirit made it clear that He wanted me to leave the formal pastorate and migrate into the business world. This is where I could engage the lost and the least churched on their turf, in their domain. Fast forward. For the next 10 years I was blessed to be highly successful in business and to enjoy the granting of my heart's desires. I was able to demonstrate and communicate the Gospel to many who would never darken the door of a church, even the most seeker friendly church. Believers who were disenfranchised from organized church began to find encouragement, shepherding and equipping in the context of the workplace. Needless to say, I was ecstatic.

My quest, though, was not ended. There began to emerge in my mind a burning question: how do these two seemingly separate parts of my life fit together? Ministry and Business. 15 years in one; 10 years in the other. Were they two different books? Two entirely distinct chapters? While I prayed about and pondered this, the Lord arranged for me to travel to Kyrgyzstan. This was the early 1990's. The Soviet Union had collapsed and Kyrgyzstan was among the many Muslim republics to break away and form independent countries. I was invited to work with the State Medical Institute to help their students learn how to establish fee-for-service medical practices in place of the collapsed centralized Soviet system. It was in Kyrgyzstan that I began to discover God's "seamless integration of business as mission." It was there as an open follower of Jesus and a real business person that the "corridors of power and influence" opened both to me and to the Gospel.

For the last 25 years it has been my privilege to operate in the space now known as BAM-- business as mission. We have launched over 1300 micro-businesses (MEDs) in 25 countries. We have helped acquire or launch several "small to midsized" enterprises (SMEs) and consulted with others. All of this is with a focus to see Jesus Christ demonstrated, communicated, and embraced in and through business around the world. This is my passion. This is my calling. This is my joy.

As a personal update, we have now begun to focus on equipping the next generation of young leaders in the BAM movement. Third Path Initiative, www.thirdpathinitiative.com, is an international consortium of universities, pastors, BAM practitioners and leaders committed to multiplying BAM resources and accelerating the BAM movement.

In 2006 my first book was published. Business as Mission: The Power of Business in the Kingdom of God. It has been very well received and I have received many notes of thanks and encouraging testimonies about how the concepts in it have helped business people find their meaningful place in God's work in the world-- especially among the unreached who live in very hard to get to places. This book takes up where Business as Mission leaves off. Specifically, this book is built on 5 bedrock principles:

1. Jesus Christ is Lord now of every sphere of life.
2. There is no Biblical distinction whatsoever between the "sacred" and "secular" callings in life.
3. All true followers of Jesus need to get out of the 4 walls of the church building and impact the world for

Christ where He has sovereignly placed us.
4. Disciples of Christ need to be totally immersed and engaged in our non-Christian society.
5. Business is just one of many spheres in which the previous 4 things can occur.

So, as you read this book, I pray that God will encourage you and help you discover that for a business person who loves Jesus there is a special place in the Kingdom and a special way in which you can impact it.

Sola Dei Gloria!

NOTE: in this book, unless otherwise noted all Scripture quotations are used from the English Standard Version, 2001, Crossway Publications.

CHAPTER 1

DISCOVERING THE NEED

My good friend, Peter Kentley, had read my first book and invited me to address the Cre8 Conference in Melbourne, Australia that year. After one of the main sessions several approached me. "We really like your book," the group said, "but it doesn't really apply directly to most of us. We're having to work really hard to make the leap. You need to write another book!" My Aussie audience in typical Aussie fashion were bringing their feedback right up the middle--which, by the way, is the how I like it. And they were right.

I have pretty much always been an entrepreneur. I started working when I was eleven and haven't stopped since. I've started service companies, consulting companies, churches, and ministries. I've normally been the founder, the CEO. And, I hate to admit, this background blinded me to an obvious truth. It's one thing to build a kingdom company, a BAM business, when you're in control. But what about the other 85% out there. As one brother put it, "What about the rest of us?" This book will help answer that question.

The fundamental principles are the same. I outlined them in Business as Mission (YWAM Publishing, 2006). Business in the kingdom is...

- Vocational--it is a high and holy calling from God on the same level as all other callings including "ministry."
- Intentional--it is to be deliberately connected to God's ultimate purpose in the world.
- Relational--it is a web of people entrusted to us by God to serve, love and develop.
- Operational--it is a business and needs to be managed in a way that glorifies God and creates a profit, i.e. financial, social and spiritual impact (a.k.a. the "triple bottom line."

Yet while the principles are the same the practical applications are quite different when you report to somebody else, when somebody else is the boss or owner, when you are what my Australian friends called "2IC" or "second in command."

Some would question if it is even possible to see a company do "business as mission" if you aren't the CEO or if there is any hope of significant kingdom impact in such a case. The answer is a strong "Yes!" I would particularly point out two men from Scripture who were clearly not the "main man" and yet no one would doubt that their presence contributed to remarkable results and kingdom outcomes--the deliverance of nations, the declaration of the glory of God, the pointing of kings to the YAHWEH, the practical blessings of many people, and even leading the CEO to confess that "the Lord He is God." Of course I'm referring to Joseph and Daniel. I call Joseph the "boy who delivered two nations." Daniel is the "boy who served as a trusted advisor to two empires." Both had tremendous impact over a long period of time. Both labored under adverse circumstances. Both saw God honored in and through their careers. I realize that none of us is Joseph or Daniel. However, we are no less than they. We are the children and servants of the Most High God and He longs to work through us too. Much of the balance of this book will be based on analysis of the lives of these two men.

One of the reasons this book has taken so

long to be written is that I didn't want to write out of theory alone--even theory based on Scripture. I need to write what I've learned from experience. To that end, I turned my consulting business over to my partner a few years ago and went to work as an employee for one of my clients. Using Joseph and Daniel as role models I have sought to see kingdom purposes affected in and through the company. The situation is different. It has unique challenges. Yet, I can say that God, in His amazing faithfulness, has proven to me that He can and will use those of us who are "second in command" or in other positions as an employee as a witness and as a catalyst to Kingdom Impact. BAM is not limited to the entrepreneur or owner; it is a calling for all of us.

CHAPTER 2

FOUNDATIONAL PRINCIPLES

Before we jump into the stories of Joseph and Daniel and the applications that arise from them, I think it would be helpful if we focused briefly on a handful of foundational principles. These truths derive from Scripture and serve to both guide and summarize our discussions of Business as Mission for both entrepreneurs and employees with a BAM mindset.

There is no "sacred-secular" divide, only one integrated Kingdom under the Limitless Lordship of Jesus Christ. No disciple of Jesus will ever enjoy the freedom God intended until we once and for all recognize and reject the historical and heretical belief that there are some things in life (ministry, missions) that are sacred and others (jobs, business, sports) that are secular. Sacred places, sacred foods, sacred buildings, sacred jobs are right up there with relics, robes and blessed steps; they are creations of man and find no support in Scripture. Indeed, in Scripture we find the sacredness of all things and all places as Jesus declares Himself Lord over them. Consider the words of Paul to the Christians in Colossae:

> For by Him all things were created in heaven and on earth, visible and invisible, whether thrones or dominions or rulers or authorities--all things were created through Him and for Him. And He is before all things, and in Him all things hold together. And He is the head of the body, the church. He is the beginning, the firstborn from the dead, that in everything He might be preeminent. For in Him all the fullness was pleased to dwell and through Him to reconcile all things, whether on earth or in heaven, making peace by the blood of His cross. (Colossians 2:16-20, ESV; italics mine)

When I was working in the UK I visited Buckingham Palace. I was surprised when my English host looked and commented that "the Queen isn't here." He went on to explain that when the Queen is in residence her flag is flying and that it wasn't flying over the palace that day. A few days later I was at Balmoral Castle in Scotland, one of the Queen's country homes. The royal flag was high above the castle. She was there. In the same way, the flag of Jesus flies wherever He is Lord and there is nowhere in heaven or earth where that flag is not powerfully waving!

Business is a good thing from God and a high and holy calling--as high as any other.

When we began teaching business in Central Asia shortly after the collapse of the Soviet Union we were surprised at not only the lack of understanding of what business is and how it works but also at the fear and suspicion that existed regarding business and business people-- especially on the part of the pastors. We addressed this by creating a pre-training for our program entitled simply "Business is a Good Thing from God" and outlined what Scripture has to say about God's plan and purpose for enterprise in His creation (pre-fall) and in His Kingdom (post-fall). From what I see and hear in churches in the West we may need to teach this material here as well. A high view of business on the part of church leaders would go a long way to empower and unleash the business people sitting in their congregations to serve Christ where He has called them.

In the same way, being in business is a high and holy calling on an equal footing with all others. Instead of a "called" and "uncalled" in the Church there are only the called (Ephesians 4:1; 1 Corinthians 1:9). Moreover, all callings are equal. There is no hierarchy or value pyramid of callings. The concept of the "priesthood of believers" makes that very clear. "You yourselves like living stones are being built up as a spiritual house, to be a holy priesthood, to offer spiritual sacrifices acceptable to God through Jesus Christ." (1 Peter 2:5, ESV; italics mine) To be sure there are different gifts and offices within the Body of Christ (Ephesians 4:11-16) but these are in function and focus not standing or status. We need a renewed emphasis on this reality if we are to see Christians effective for the Kingdom in the marketplace and around the world.

Business and career, like all things, should be intentionally connected to what God is doing in the world. The Great Commission applies to all of us. It is not just for pastors or missionaries.

The Grand Purpose of God, the discipling of the nations and the filling of the earth with those who love, honor and obey Him has been in place from the beginning. It was God's purpose in the Garden of Eden when He told Adam and Eve to "be fruitful and multiply and fill the earth." (Genesis 1:28) It was reiterated in the commissioning of Abram (Abraham) in Genesis 12:1-3. And, of course, Jesus republished it after His resurrection saying, "All authority in heaven and on earth has been given to me. Go therefore and make disciples of all nations, baptizing them in the name of the Father and of the Son and of the Holy Spirit, teaching them to observe all that I have commanded you. And behold, I am with you always, to the end of the age." (Matthew 28:18-20, ESV)

This is what God is doing in the world. And we, all of us, are to be a part of that. We are to be deliberately connected, strategically connected to God's plan. Business is no exception. In fact, in my opinion, the sine qua non of Business as Mission is just that--the intentional connection of my company, my job, my career to the Great Commission...at home and globally.

Let me make a point. While Business as Mission does not require leaving home and doing business cross-culturally as some maintain I do believe that in the grand scheme of things we, particularly Christians in the West, need to take a hard look at the rest of the world, at the developing nations, and especially unreached people groups. As late as this year, 95% of the unreached and least reached live in a clearly defined geography that includes North Africa, the Middle East, and South and Southeast Asia. They are primarily Muslim, Hindu, Buddhists, and Communist Atheists. Shockingly, however, only 5% of the resources of the Christian community are active in those same geographies. While these statistics do not compel me to go they should at least compel me to ask if I should or if my business can somehow make a difference among those people.

Kingdom Impact is not limited to individual conversions. It includes all manner of blessings that bring mercy, health, and benefits to society. One of the reasons that modern Christians tend to think with a defeatist mentality is that we have limited the definition of the Kingdom and Kingdom Impact to basically the matters of individual salvation. To be sure, the Christian experience begins with a personal relationship with Jesus Christ; this can never be over-emphasized. As my old mentor used to say, "Christianity is Christ."

Yet Christ is much more than just a personal Savior. He is also the great Healer, the King, the Shepherd, the Provider, the Guide. He is the source of all that is good in the world and desires nothing but good for the world. He is the Benefactor. He is the Redeemer. He is the Liberator. He is the Judge who delivers the oppressed. He is the Friend of the friendless, the Hope of the hopeless, the Refuge in the time of storm. In a phrase, Jesus is the Restorer of all things to God and the Transformer of society.

Consequently, when a person is drawn to saving faith in Christ that is Kingdom Impact. At the same time, when a hungry man is fed or a homeless family sheltered that is also Kingdom Impact. Likewise, the unemployed given gainful work, the outcast embraced, the leper healed, the fractured mended and the grieving comforted. All of these are expressions of God's Kingdom in action. The cup of cold water or the clothing of the naked or the visit to the prisoner are not without meaning to Jesus. (Matthew 25:41-45). Jesus explained what the Kingdom actually is when He taught us to pray in what we often call "The Lord's Prayer." Note the words:

Our Father Who art in heaven,
Hallowed be Thy name.
Thy kingdom come,
(that is) Thy will be done on
earth as it is in heaven..."
(Matthew 6 9-10, KJV)

Where the will of God is done there is the
Kingdom of God. Where is that? Only in personal
conversion? No. Also in deeds of mercy, kindness,
generosity, peacemaking, and reconciliation. Until
we broaden our understanding of the Kingdom
our measuring of our own usefulness in any
context (and especially in business) will be
warped, our vision stunted and our enjoyment of
seeing God's hand in the world minimized.

The Equipping Ministry of pastors and
teachers and others within the Body of
Christ is to enable us to do service outside
the four walls. The ministries referred to in
Ephesians 4:11-15 are not just to help us
perform better Christmas cantatas or teach
better Sunday School classes or provide
better AV. The 4-fold ministries (apostle,
prophet, evangelist and pastor-teacher) are
in place to train, encourage and empower
the other gifted ministers in the church for

service both inside and outside the church. In other words, pastors exist to raise up the entrepreneur, the manager, the physician, the academic, the homemaker, the neighbor, the farmer and the scientist so that they can effectively serve Christ where He has called and placed us--on the other side of the stained glass windows!

When people in the world of business begin to grasp their high and holy calling and the duly appointed teachers and shepherds of the Body focus on providing them what they need to fulfill that calling, I believe, we will see what Billy Graham said many years ago: I believe that one of the next great moves of God is going to be through the believers in the workplace.[1]

Conclusion

As we transition into the guts of this book, please keep these five foundational building blocks in the back of your mind. From time to time it may be helpful to return

---

[1] Billy Graham quoted by Mark Whitaker, TwoTen Magazine, Issue 5, 4Q 2013, online version.

to this chapter and review them. They are Scriptural reminders, signposts, that will help us find our way.

CHAPTER 3

DANIEL: THE BOY WHO GREW UP TO IMPACT TWO EMPIRES

The Story in Short

It was the year 605 BC--dark times for Judah and especially for the capital city of Jerusalem. The forces of Babylon, the world superpower, are in the process of conquering and absorbing the once proud kingdom of David. One king after of another was deposed and replaced as Nebuchadnezzar systematically dismantled Israel.

Part of Nebuchadnezzar's foreign policy was to gradually change the culture of conquered territories so that, over time, they would come to think and act like Babylonians. One of the ways he did this was by taking the very best and brightest young minds of the defeated lands and bringing to Babylon to be educated in the ways of the Babylonians and to learn their language (a major vehicle for cultural change). At the same time, Nebuchadnezzar would gain the energy and insight of every nation he captured, thus making Babylon stronger than ever.

It is in this setting that we meet a 14-year-old boy named Daniel. Daniel was among those chosen by the Babylonians for re-education. This group is described in Scripture as being of "the royal family and of the nobility, youths without blemish, of good appearance and skillful in all wisdom, endowed with knowledge, understanding learning…" (Daniel 1:3-4, ESV) They were the cream of the crop and as such given access to the corridors of education and power.

In Babylon Daniel immediately began to set himself apart as someone to watch (Daniel 1:19). We are familiar with the events of his life--his refusal to defile himself with pagan foods (Daniel 1), his ability to interpret dreams (Daniel 2 and 4), his rise to prominence in the court of Nebuchadnezzar and to remain as a strategic advisor to Belshazzar, the descendent of Nebuchadnezzar and the son of King Nabonidus. This last point is important because it demonstrates something special about Daniel. It is one thing to become an advisor to a king but to more than one, and in this case several, is extremely rare. But then Daniel was a rare individual.

At the end of the reign of Belshazzar Babylon was overrun by the Medo-Persians (the night of the famous "handwriting on the wall" in Daniel 5) and a new empire assumed the role of world superpower. And where was Daniel? In the seat of a trusted counselor to King Darius. It is entirely possible to derive from the narrative the idea that Daniel went into obscurity for a period and was then recalled to service under Darius; he may have simply remained in the inner circle. Either way, Daniel established himself as a player in more than one empire!

In this new political setting Daniel was once again tested and once again risked his life in order to remain faithful to God. His refusal to stop praying in the Hebrew way as decreed by Darius led to his well known encounter with the Lion's Den (Daniel 6) and the miraculous deliverance we have heard about since Sunday School days.

The story of Daniel's amazing life begins to dim after this. There is only a reference to his continued impact on Darius and his son, Cyrus the Great. "So this Daniel prospered during the reign of Darius and the reign of Cyrus the Persian." (Daniel 6:28)

At some point, Daniel died. We don't know when (Cyrus died in 530 BC) and it doesn't really matter. We do know how he lived and how God used this young boy to become a trusted advisor to multiple kings and kingdoms and to bring glory to the LORD for decades--all in the most adverse of circumstances.

The Lessons

I hope you can see why I would choose Daniel as one of our examples of impacting an organization, be it government, military, or company, for God and seeing demonstrable Kingdom Impact when you are not the boss. Prophets we can understand. Kings also. But exiled children? Government employees? Those who are, at best, "second in command?" Daniel is more than an example to us, to the rest of us; he is an inspiration and a kind of "patron saint."

There are three great lessons to be seen in Daniel's life and work. These will form the outline of the next section:

1. Daniel's place was God's place for him.

2. Daniel's life confirmed the reality of his faith.

3. Daniel's words pointed men to God.

CHAPTER 4

LESSON ONE: DANIEL'S PLACE WAS GOD'S PLACE FOR HIM

> In the third year of the reign of Jehoiakim king of Judah, Nebuchadnezzar king of Babylon came to Jerusalem and besieged it. And the Lord gave Jehoiakim king of Judah into his hand, with some of the vessels of the house of God. And he brought them to the land of Shinar, to the house of his god, and placed the vessels in the treasury of his god. Then the king commanded Ashpenaz, his chief eunuch, to bring some of the people of Israel, both of the royal family and of the nobility... (Daniel 1: 1-4, ESV)

Have you ever sat down in your office or reported to the job site on a Monday morning or headed to the airport and found yourself wondering, "How did I ever get here?" or "Lord, does any of this stuff really matter?" I certainly have--and I did it even when I was in the "ministry!" I don't think anyone in any role is immune to this kind of thinking and self-questioning. In fact, the more you care about honoring God in your life the more you probably ask these kind of things.

It's not in the Biblical record but I strongly suspect Daniel asked these same things. Certainly he did in the early days of his captivity and re-education. It would be superhuman not to. Perhaps over the years he learned the first lesson for himself, i.e. that his place was God's place for him.

Even though Daniel was not where he would have chosen to be he was where God chose for him to be...and in that place is where God used him.

There are many ways to look at Daniel's situation. We might call it a tragedy--to be torn from home and family at such a young age. We might call it imperialism--the thoughtless bullying of a superpower over a weaker one. We might call it bad luck--being in the wrong place at the wrong time. We might even somehow try to attribute it to bad choices that Daniel or his parents made. Of course, none of these is correct and none offers any hope or instruction for us.

The simple truth is that God placed Daniel in Babylon. There was no chance, no geopolitical root cause. There was, as there is today, the sovereign hand of God executing His plan in all things (Ephesians 1:11). No doubt, Daniel was not where he would have chosen to be. He did not sign up for it, pray for it or lobby to be "selected." This was part of God's divine design--not just for Daniel but also for Israel and the world.

So Daniel was where God placed him. Arguing or whining couldn't and wouldn't change that. God's will is God's will. Period. And perfect (Romans 12:2) To accept that is part of being a servant of Christ. And here's the really good news. Not only was Daniel in God's place for him but it is also in that place that God would use him. Today, many of us spend an enormous amount of energy lost in "if only" thinking. If only I were somewhere else. If only I worked at another company. If only... This is a highly effective trap of the enemy that keeps the followers of Jesus absorbed with their circumstances instead of God's choice. We, like Daniel, are exactly where God wants us and it is here that He will use us. Can I repeat that to make my point? It is where God has placed us that He will use! If that is what we most want then one of our greatest challenges is to accept and embrace His choice.

Now the question of God's choice opens the door to think about God's calling, a.k.a., the "doctrine of vocation." The word for call in Greek is kaleo. In the context of the New Testament it means "a divine invitation that comes with authority." In other words, the call of God is a choice to accept but not to ignore. It may be arguable as in the case of Moses but it is ultimately inescapable. If you question that I suggest you make a note to have a talk with Jonah when you get to heaven.

And we are used to thinking this way in certain circumstances. When someone accepts the call to the pastorate or to be a foreign missionary we are very comfortable with the terminology, "I surrendered. to…"

But what about the rest of us. Are we without call? Are we the uncalled? The booming answer from Scripture is "No!" All of the people of God are called. Abraham was. David was. Daniel was. Paul was. Lazarus was. And you are. There are no uncalled--at least not in the Scriptural sense. Consider 1 Corinthians 1:9 and Ephesians

4:1 for starters. Especially think through this passage:

> Only let each person lead the life that the Lord has assigned to him, and to which God has called him. This is my rule in all the churches. (1 Corinthians 7:17, ESV)

> Each one should remain in the condition in which he was called. Were you a bondservant when called? Do not be concerned about it. (1 Corinthians 7:19-20, ESV)

> So, brothers, in whatever condition each was called, there let him remain with God. (1 Corinthians 7:24, ESV)

It is critical, once and for all, that the Church embrace and teach the doctrine of vocation so that those in business or any other profession feel and enjoy the confidence that comes from knowing "I am called by God to this or that."

An important corollary to the joyful reality that you and I are called and placed where God wants us--one brother called this "theography"--is that there is no hierarchy in callings. There are no good callings and bad callings, high callings and low callings. The great doctrine of the Priesthood of all Believers makes it clear that we all stand equal in the Body of Christ and that we are not victims of some ecclesiastical caste system.

When my wife and I were in missionary training school many years ago we along with all the students learned of a particular pecking order in the Kingdom. It wasn't taught by the faculty but it surely was caught by everyone. To this day, if you ask any graduate you will get an answer that runs something like this:

1. If you really love God and are very special to Him He will call you to be a missionary. That's the crème de la crème. Top shelf.
2. If you love God and you are special you can be a pastor. Decent posting.
3. If you sort of love God and you are average then the caring professions are

for you--nursing, being a doctor or teacher, etc. Honorable role.

4. For the rest of us there's business--get a job or perhaps start a company-- through which you prove your worth by financially supporting the others.

I usually get a good laugh when I share this at a conference but it's a laugh based on irony. This is pretty much what Christians believe and it leaves business people in a very sad place of thinking, deep in their hearts, if only I could be in ministry or if only God had called me to the mission field. And even within the business world we are thinking in terms of levels when we elevate the entrepreneurs above employees in their relative calling in and value to the cause of Christ.

Enter Daniel, a man clearly called of God but not as a missionary and not as a pastor and not as a teacher or physician. A government advisor. A government advisor used by God to help lead two world superpowers and described as "a man greatly beloved" of God. (Daniel 9:23, KJV)

How desperately the Body of Christ needs to recover the lost truth of the Priesthood of all Believers. For all of God's people and especially those in the business to realize that we are indeed called by God and placed by God in His perfect will into the exact business setting that we occupy would cause our chains of remorse and false guilt to fall off. To accept that the call to business is exactly as important and as high in God's estimation as the missionary call would enable Christians in the marketplace (domestically and internationally) to lift up their heads, spread their wings and soar joyfully into the work that the Lord has specifically prepared them to do for Him (Ephesians 2:10)

It is hard to run a race looking over your shoulder with glances of self-doubt. If only I were in the "ministry" or "where did I miss the path?" Instead, when we realize this lesson from Daniel's life and see it throughout the Word, our heart is freed. We can "press on toward the goal for the prize of the upward call of God in Christ Jesus." (Philippians 3:14 ESV) We can give ourselves with utter and joyful abandon to

God's will, to God's plan, to God's place and serve the Lord with gladness in the world of business.

CHAPTER 5

LESSON ONE: DANIEL'S LIFE CONFIRMED HIS FAITH

If you forget everything else in this chapter, please remember this: the world needs to see the gospel as much as it needs to hear it. Depending on where you live, you might even conclude that folks have already heard the gospel--a lot of gospel, via radio, TV, church attendance, college ministries, etc. In those situations, (especially in the West), the issue is not so much hearing the claims of Christianity as it is seeing the reality of Christianity. Even in the toughest places among the least reached and unreached seeing is equally as important as hearing. Imagine Daniel's professions of the Hebrew faith without the life to go with it. Thankfully that is not what happened. Daniel's life was in sync with his faith, demonstrated the reality of his faith and confirmed the truth of his words. In other words, Daniel was authentic.

What the World Needs to See

"Your life is so loud I can't hear what you are

saying" is a phrase often thrown in the faces of Christians. Even though it is often just a weak excuse for rejecting Jesus it is still true enough that we need to listen. Mahatmas Gandhi once remarked that "were it not for the Christians I have met I might have been one." I, for one, grew up in the church and never "saw" the gospel; I "heard" it but never really heard it in part because I never saw it. It was not until a true follower of Jesus became my friend in university that I saw Christianity in someone's life and was consequently open to hearing the message. My life has been forever changed by what I saw. Thank you, Richard!

Now let's be clear on what the world needs to see. They don't need to see "Churchianity." They don't need to see the collection of evangelical-pharisaical practices many identify with following Jesus--bumper stickers, fish symbols, Christian jewelry, "Christianese," going to church, or carrying Bibles.

Jesus said that love and unity would be the visible signs of our faith and His Lordship (John 13:34-35; 17:21). Believe it or not, these traits are as meaningful in the business setting as they are in the neighborhood. They can never be argued with or refuted. They cannot be ignored.

There are two other traits I've seen that make the world sit up and take notice. The first is excellence of character (an extension of love). The second is excellence of work (perhaps an extension of love also). These stand out in the corporate world, in the market place, in any culture and any land. There simply is no argument against these and Daniel had them both.

Excellent character is coupled with excellent work. One leads to the other. Who can find fault with that? A truly good man doing truly good work. I remember many years back I had a boss-- before I had even begun to think about Business as Mission--who asked me what my career goals were. Like many a young buck I answered, "I want your job." He was the founder, owner and CEO so clearly I didn't lack in ambition--humility perhaps but not ambition. I quickly added, "Even I can't ever be CEO like you I'd still like to be capable of doing your job." Continuous learning with the goal of excellence is something I believe in and something I look for in new hires and candidates for promotion.

Think about this narrative based on the

opinions of Daniel's peers:

> Then this Daniel became distinguished above all the other high officials and satraps, because an excellent spirit was in him. And the king planned to set him over the whole kingdom. Then the high officials and the satraps sought to find a ground for complaint against Daniel with regard to the kingdom, but they could find no ground for complaint or any fault, because he was faithful, and no error or fault was found in him. Then these men said, "We shall not find any ground for complaint against this Daniel unless we find it in connection with the law of his God." (Daniel 6:3-5 ESV)

Much like when Jesus was on trial and His accusers could find no fault in Him--even when they conspired to lie in order to have Him executed--Daniel's enemies were stumped when it came to finding grounds to accuse him before the king. And don't you know they tried! Have you ever had a coworker who was jealous of you or threatened by you or passed over in favor of you? If you have then you know the kind of venomous hatred these men had for Daniel. Yet Daniel lived his faith in such a practical and observable way he stymied his enemies. What's more, as we shall see in just a moment, he impressed his "boss." Excellence in character and excellence in work may lead to the Lions' Den or Calvary but is never ignored!

I wonder, with low expectations, if people looking at me at work would quickly use the phrase "excellence of character" or "excellence of work" to describe me. I wonder, with an even greater sense of inadequacy, if they would conclude that the only fault they could find in me would be in the fact that I refuse to compromise my commitment to Christ!

When Excellence Prevails

Life is not fair. No place is this reality more pronounced than in business. Not every excellent man or woman doing excellent work and producing excellent results will rise as Daniel did but most will. Even in the face of persecution excellence is extremely difficult to ignore or overlook. It was certainly the case with Daniel.

After one of his earliest demonstrations of

faith in front of King Nebuchadnezzar we read these words:

> Then King Nebuchadnezzar fell upon his face and paid homage to Daniel, and commanded that an offering and incense be offered up to him. The king answered and said to Daniel, "Truly, your God is God of gods and Lord of kings, and a revealer of mysteries, for you have been able to reveal this mystery." Then the king gave Daniel high honors and many great gifts, and made him ruler over the whole province of Babylon and chief prefect over all the wise men of Babylon. (Daniel 2:46-48 ESV)

In Daniel 5 we see this again:

> Then Belshazzar gave the command, and Daniel was clothed with purple, a chain of gold was put around his neck, and a proclamation was made about him, that he should be the third ruler in the kingdom. (Daniel 5:29 ESV)

Note that in this passage, Daniel's promotion

under King Belshazzar came after an excellent performance delivering terrible news! And under two more kings, Daniel's excellence of character and work led to promotion, respect and prosperity:

> So this Daniel prospered during the reign of Darius and the reign of Cyrus the Persian. (Daniel 6:28 ESV)

Make a note of this. It is true that Daniel's character and work and authentic expression of his faith resulted in regular and dramatic promotions (something most of us desire in our jobs) they also, and infinitely more importantly, communicated in undeniable ways that Yahweh was real and that He alone was the true and living God. Isn't this what our deepest heart longs for? I want to be recognized. I want to be rewarded. Yet, more than anything, I desire to see Jesus Christ uplifted and honored and known among my colleagues and employees. As we have all, no doubt, said many times, I long to know Him and make Him known.

Words without excellence, words without character, words without solid work will not bring that about. Only real faith expressed in real ways will. Daniel's real faith expressed in real ways led pagan kings to fall on their faces and proclaim for all their empire to hear: The LORD, He is God! Listen to the words of one of them:

> Then King Darius wrote to all the peoples, nations, and languages that dwell in all the earth: "Peace be multiplied to you. I make a decree, that in all my royal dominion people are to tremble and fear before the God of Daniel, for he is the living God, enduring forever; his kingdom shall never be destroyed, and his dominion shall be to the end. He delivers and rescues; he works signs and wonders in heaven and on earth, he who has saved Daniel from the power of the lions." (Daniel 6:25-27 ESV)

Conclusion

Religion is irrelevant. Ritual and rote, veneer and symbols, "spiritual practices"--these mean nothing to the lost executive in the corner office and they mean nothing to the Muslim merchant in North Africa. Only reality matters. Only the truth proclaimed and embodied in the lives of the followers of Christ in the power of the Holy Spirit can change lives and bring about true gospel witness. It has always been so. (1 Corinthians 2:1-5)

I was traveling back from California with a client when our plane was diverted to Houston because of mechanical issues. When we landed, he and I went to find a coffee shop to while away the time. Within a few minutes, the client wanted to know if he could ask me a personal question. "Sure," I said. He then emphasized that he meant really personal. I agreed. He asked, "I want to know what this fire, this passion is inside of you." When I asked in return if he really wanted to know he said emphatically "Yes!" I began, "The passion in me that you see is Jesus Christ..." He interrupted, "I knew it!" From then until our plane was boarded some two hours later we had an amazing discussion about what it meant to know Jesus in a personal way. From his South American Roman Catholic background he found this hard to understand but he was interested, very interested. He walked closely with me as we boarded, still asking questions and as we were seated he asked the woman next to me if she would change seats with him so we could continue our conversation. All in all, for about 4 hours, this lost client opened his heart to learn about salvation and following Christ.

In another encounter in Canada, having just finished the second of a five-day course on statistical process control (SPC), I was approached by the plant manager. He wanted to have dinner that night. I agreed and then asked why. Tommy said, "Because you know God and I don't." Now I can assure you that there is nothing particularly exciting or spiritual about statistical process control and I'm not one to lace teaching or coaching with "God references." Nevertheless, something in my life resonated with Tommy and that evening a hopeless alcoholic heard the life changing gospel of Jesus Christ for the first time.

My favorite story of the power of authentic living is not mine; it is one of our students. In the early 2000's, our volunteer based micro enterprise team had helped launch a series of small, Kingdom-focused businesses in various parts of Indonesia. As part of our process we require participants to write a Kingdom Impact Statement spelling out how their new business will connect to God's work in the world. Joseph (not his real name for obvious reasons) said that he wanted to open an auto repair shop (not his real business) in his village and do such quality of work with such a great attitude that his Muslim neighbors would know that Jesus is Lord. Within a year, the imam of the local mosque announced to his congregation, "There is only one place that I can recommend to have your car worked on. Joseph the Christian's shop."

My friends, if you are serious about Kingdom impact in your work setting, particularly if you are not the boss, then devote yourself to the development of excellent character and the delivery of excellent work. Ditch the symbols and the veneer. Jettison the pious words. Live among the lost as Jesus did and watch God work!

CHAPTER 6

LESSON THREE: DANIEL'S WORDS POINTED MEN TO GOD

In the last chapter I emphasized Daniel's life. Like all things if taken out of context you might conclude that I think actions and good deeds are a sufficient witness and enough to bring men to a saving knowledge of Christ. I don't. I believe that people need to hear the word of God as much as they need to see the works of God. Seeing may support believing but saving faith ultimately comes by hearing the truth of the gospel. (Romans 10:17)

The world of work is a wide open mission field both at home and in cross-cultural settings. In the increasingly postmodern West men and women desperately need to hear the message of Christ and that witness will most likely occur in the marketplace. Among the least reached and unreached men and women desperately need to hear the gospel and that will also often happen within the context of a business transaction or relationship. You and I, like Daniel, are uniquely and strategically positioned to be that message bearer, that story teller, that gospel witness. Can I be very specific? That person in the cubicle next to you or in the office down the hall or out in the warehouse or in the branch in another town may not even know a single follower of Jesus. You are where you are at the behest of our sovereign God to be able to reach out to that person and to let your words, like your life, point him or her to Jesus!

What Not to Do

Sadly, the vast majority of Christians will live out their entire lives without sharing the gospel with one person! Others, just as sadly will make the effort but they come across in such a way as to be, as one friend of mine in Australia called them, the "anti-evangelists." Let's not replace one travesty with another.

One of my favorite words is obstreperous. It means unnecessarily difficult, offensive, and awkward. Don't be obstreperous when you share the redemption message. Over the years I have had Christians describe the persecution they experience in the workplace or in their neighborhood "for the gospel's sake." As I probe and find out more of what is happening I say to them, "You are not suffering for being a Christian.

You are suffering for being a jerk!" I don't know where they learned evangelism but somewhere along the way they lost the main point that evangelism literally means "good newsing" and not "religiously offending."

Here's one example of what I mean: the damners. Zealous disciples often approach their victims with an aggressive and confrontational demeanor. Turn or burn! Cry or fry! Somehow their flavor of Christianity revolves around telling people what horrible sinners they are. The more aggressive the better. Many years ago, while still in seminary, I heard Rick Warren say something to the effect that telling people they are sinners is not the good news; in fact it's not even news at all. They know they are sinners (even if they don't use that word or other correct theological language). What I need to hear is God's way of salvation. Lovingly sharing both the standard of God (i.e. the Law) and the work of Christ (i.e. the gospel) is entirely, historically and redemptively sufficient! Followers of Jesus, remember that our Master only approximated harshness when dealing with self-righteous Pharisees!

Then there are the debaters. When I was first saved I had a habit of trying to argue people into the kingdom. I would debate and debunk until finally my intellectual targets caved in and fell mentally exhausted into the Kingdom--not! I finally faced the real issue one day when, midway through a strong apologetic discussion, I asked my sparring partner, "So, if I can prove to you beyond doubt that Jesus rose from the dead will you trust and follow Him?" He replied, "No." Right then and there I began to understand that rejection of the gospel is not an intellectual problem solved with highly developed arguments; the problem with the lost is that they are lost, dead in their sins and spiritually unable to believe until the Holy Spirit quickens them. Here's Paul's description:

> And you were dead in the trespasses and sins...But God, being rich in mercy, because of the great love with which he loved us, even when we were dead in our trespasses, made us alive together with Christ—by grace you have been saved— (Ephesians 2:1, 4-5 ESV)

Being right only salves my ego. It doesn't raise the dead! That's God's work.

There are the dutiful. Sharing the gospel is not a joy or a privilege or an overflow of our vital connection to Christ. It is duty. It's what you do. It's what is commanded, prescribed, and demanded. Evangelism is driven by guilt and obligation. So, with all the attractiveness of a child told to go clean up his room the dutiful believer "shares the good news." It's patently clear to whomever he or she is witnessing to that this is a royal pain in the rear and not coming from a place of humility, love or compassion.

And finally there are the data collectors. My oldest daughter quickly emerged as one of the leaders of a campus ministry organization while in college. She was leading Bible studies and sharing her faith with her friends. Soon she was asked to be the leader on campus. She refused. When I asked her why she told me, "Daddy, they want me to turn in weekly reports of how many people I witnessed to, how many accepted Christ and how many attended my Bible studies and I just won't do that." Bravo! If the motivation in sharing Christ is to be able to return to the Ponderosa and "show and tell" what you've done how can that selfish motivation not come through to the world?

Daniel's Witness

Studying the account of Daniel reveals several important things for those of us who labor in the marketplace. From a place of not being in charge Daniel was still a powerful and effective witness for God.

First, Daniel was none of the above. Daniel was bold. Daniel was true. However, he was never rude. He was never argumentative. He wasn't keeping score. The truth of his message may have been offensive as the gospel often is but he wasn't.

Second, Daniel was not silent. When given the chance Daniel spoke. He earned the right to be heard and he spoke to be heard. I am deeply concerned when Christians in business are mute about Jesus. Are you "living" it and not "speaking" it? This challenge applies to believers in their home market and it equally applies to those who move to work in foreign lands. Let's be clear. Going to the mission field does not make someone a missionary.

Third, Daniel was opportunistic, clear and focused on God. On multiple occasions, set up by his life and faithfulness, Daniel "redeemed the time." (Ephesians 5:15, KJV)

Prior to interpreting Nebuchadnezzar's dream (Daniel's first big break) he immediate points the king to God:

> Daniel answered the king and said, "No wise men, enchanters, magicians, or astrologers can show to the king the mystery that the king has asked, but there is a God in heaven who reveals mysteries, and he has made known to King Nebuchadnezzar what will be in the latter days. Your dream and the visions of your head as you lay in bed are these: To you, O king, as you lay in bed came thoughts of what would be after this, and he who reveals mysteries made known to you what is to be. But as for me, this mystery has been revealed to me, not because of any wisdom that I have more than all the living, but in order that the interpretation may be made known to the king, and that you may know the thoughts of your mind. (Daniel 2:27-30 ESV)

Talk about blowing the interview! And after interpreting the king's dream Daniel doesn't stop. Without flinching or apology Daniel explains, "A great God has made known to the king what shall be after this. The dream is certain, and its interpretation sure." (Daniel 2:45 ESV)

On another occasion and after interpreting another of Nebuchadnezzar's visions Daniel puts it all on the line with these words:

> ...this is the interpretation, O king: It is a decree of the Most High, which has come upon my lord this is the interpretation, O king: It is a decree of the Most High, which has come upon my lord the king, that you shall be driven from among men, and your dwelling shall be with the beasts of the field. You shall be made to eat grass like an ox, and you shall be wet with the dew of heaven, and seven periods of time shall pass over you, till you know that the Most High rules the kingdom of men and gives it to whom he will. And as it was commanded to leave the stump of the roots of the tree, your kingdom shall be confirmed for

you from the time that you know that Heaven rules. Therefore, O king, let my counsel be acceptable to you: break off your sins by practicing righteousness, and your iniquities by showing mercy to the oppressed, that there may perhaps be a lengthening of your prosperity." (Daniel 4:24-27 ESV)

What a wonderfully clear message. You are in big trouble because of your pride. You need to repent and acknowledge that the LORD He is God!

Once again, consider Daniel's clear and respectful testimony to King Darius after the Lord spared him in the Lions' Den:

Then, at break of day, the king arose and went in haste to the den of lions. As he came near to the den where Daniel was, he cried out in a tone of anguish. The king declared to Daniel, "O Daniel, servant of the living God, has your God, whom you serve continually, been able to deliver you from the lions?" Then Daniel said to the king, "O king, live forever! My

God sent his angel and shut the lions' mouths, and they have not harmed me, because I was found blameless before him; and also before you, O king, I have done no harm." (Daniel 6:19-22 ESV)

Have you ever found yourself in an opportunity to give an unforced acknowledgement to God in front of co-workers or the boss? What did you do? How did you do it? I want to be more like Daniel.

Following Daniel's Example

So how can we apply this specifically today? Let me suggest a few very specific action items for the follower of Jesus who would "dare to be a Daniel" in the workplace:

1. We need a very solid understanding of the Word of God and its key teachings.

    For all the years some of us have spent in Bible reading and Bible studies, for all the countless hours we've heard sermons or read books about the Bible here's haunting question: do we know it? Do we know the key things the Scriptures say and teach? Do we know what is vital versus ancillary? Are we memorizing verses and pondering their meaning? I am not asking if we are scholars or even experts. I am asking whether we are prepared to communicate the message of Christ when we get the chance. The admonition of Paul to Timothy is still valid and timely:

> All Scripture is breathed out by God and profitable for teaching, for reproof, for correction, and for training in righteousness, that the man of God may be complete, equipped for every good work. (2 Timothy 3:15-16, ESV)

2. We need a clear and simple method of sharing the gospel.

There are many well developed methods of making sure you share the gospel in an understandable way. A few I have found helpful are the Navigators "Bridge Illustration," Evangelism Explosion, and the good old "Romans Road." Regardless of the method, let's be clear on the message. Paul summarizes the essence of the gospel message, the good news in 1 Corinthians 15.

> Now I would remind you, brothers, of the gospel I preached to you, which you received, in which you stand, and by which you are being saved, if you hold fast to the word I preached to you—unless you believed in vain. For I delivered to you as of first importance what I also received: that Christ died for our sins in accordance with the Scriptures, that he was buried, that he was raised on the third day in accordance with the Scriptures...
> (1 Corinthians 15:1-4)

The gospel is simple and powerful (Romans 1:16). It is the story, the message, the news that the Son of God died for our sins, that He was buried and that God raised Him from the dead. When that message is communicated the Holy Spirit convicts of the need for a Savior and generates saving faith and evangelical repentance in the heart.

3. We need to pray regularly for opportunities to point men to God and the courage to do so when the time comes.

There is no need to force conversations or manipulate them. Daniel never did. Opportunities came to him by the sovereign hand of God and he responded to them. That means pray. Our five minutes with God rushing into our work day is simply not enough time to wait before Him and to seek His fullness, to seek Him and to ask for divine appointments. We'll look at this principle of prayer in greater detail in the chapter on the Practices of the 2IC.

4. We need to develop the personal habit of a simple "thank you" for praise and refuse to embrace glory that belongs to God.

I remember in my pastoral days the agony of standing at the door of the church and hearing repeatedly "Great sermon, pastor...changed my life...awesome!" Two things made this hard. First, I was never sure how to respond--do I say, "Praise the Lord?" Or "God is good?" Or "Yeah, I know?" Second, I knew that about half of the folks that were walking by didn't have the foggiest clue what I had even said that morning much less were they changed by it! So, finally I developed the habit of simply saying, "Thanks." If someone thought I was stealing God's glory so be it. I wasn't and if we had any chance to talk beyond the "glorification of the worm ceremony" (as Prof Hendricks called it) I'd make certain to point them to God. The same practices apply at work--it's OK to acknowledge the recognition for a job well done. Just don't bask in it. Move on and, if it's appropriate take the opportunity to give honor to the Lord.

5. We need to ask the Lord to give us His holy compassion for the lost and broken of this world.

There is simply no substitute for compassion. Jesus had it. Paul had it. Daniel had it. Do I? Do you? Do we weep over the lost? Do our hearts break for the broken? A true, humble love for those we work with is the greatest and least resistible bridge we can ever build to those outside of the faith. I don't care whether you are an employee in a multinational company living in Saudi Arabia, the only employee in a small business in China or the receptionist of a company in Sydney or New York City. If you don't really love the lost they will know it. If you do they will know that too!

Conclusion

So we see Daniel's words, like his life, pointed men to God. He lived the truth and he spoke the truth. And on at least one such occasion, Daniel's life and words led to a pagan emperor confessing the majesty of the LORD:

> Then King Nebuchadnezzar fell upon his face and paid homage to Daniel, and commanded that an offering and incense be offered up to him. The king answered and said to Daniel, "Truly, your God is God of gods and Lord of kings, and a revealer of mysteries, for

you have been able to reveal this mystery." (Daniel 2:46-47, ESB)

How would you like to see that happen where you work?

CHAPTER 7

JOSEPH: THE YOUNG MAN WHO BECAME A SLAVE AND A PRISONER AND SAVED TWO NATIONS

I have many heroes in Scripture--Peter, David, Daniel to name a few. One of them is Joseph. There is something about this young man and his journey from arrogance to devastation to greatness that inspires me. He is also a marvelous example of how God uses people who are not in charge, who are not the boss. He is, to paraphrase Tony Yeo, someone who demonstrates how to lead while still being under another's authority (Leading from the Second Chair, 2012, Tony Yeo).

Joseph's Journey

The story of Joseph begins in the late 20th century BC where he appears as one of only two sons born to Jacob and his beloved wife Rachel. (Genesis 35:24) It is explicitly stated that Joseph grew up as the favorite of Jacob's (Genesis 37:1-4) and that family dysfunction combined with Joseph's own hubris created a jealousy on the part of his brothers sets the stage for a great drama.

(Genesis 37:5-11)

When the chance presented itself, the brothers conspired to kill Joseph and tell Jacob that a wild animal had killed him. Reuben, one of the brothers, managed to persuade the others to spare his life and planned to later rescue him. However, before Reuben could stop it the other brothers sold Joseph as a slave to Midianite caravan passing by on its way to Egypt. (Genesis 37: 12-35)

The hand of God begins to be clearly seen as young Joseph ended up serving in the household of one of Pharaoh's officers (Genesis 37:36) where he quickly rose to a place of prominence, authority, and trust. In fact, he became the manager of all of Potiphar's business. (Genesis 39:1-6). However, in a story all too familiar, this impressive young man became the object of Potiphar's wife's amorous attention. Repeatedly she propositioned Joseph only to be rebuffed--no doubt a humiliating experience for her to be rejected by anyone, much less a slave. With one last desperate attempt, she approached Joseph only to be turned away again and this time Joseph fled leaving his robe behind in her hands. In the often misquoted words of William Congreve,

"Heav'n has no rage like love to hatred turn'd. Nor Hell a fury, like a woman scorn'd." And so it is with Potiphar's wife. Her attraction turned to distraction and in her anger she falsely accused Joseph of attempted rape, a charge which landed him in prison. (Genesis 39:7-20)

Yet once again we see God's blessing as Joseph gained favor in the eyes of the warden and became a trusted manager even in the prison. What an amazing testimony:

> But the LORD was with Joseph and showed him steadfast love and gave him favor in the sight of the keeper of the prison. And the keeper of the prison put Joseph in charge of all the prisoners who were in the prison. Whatever was done there, he was the one who did it. The keeper of the prison paid no attention to anything that was in Joseph's charge, because the LORD was with him. And whatever he did, the LORD made it succeed.(Genesis 37:21-23, ESV)

This pattern actually becomes a paradigm for Joseph's life. Adversity landed him in slavery;

character, ability and the grace of God raised him to responsibility in Potiphar's household. Adversity sent him to prison; God's blessing brought him right back to a place of influence and impact.

In prison, Joseph's restoration began when he interpreted the dreams of two prisoners who were fallen servants of Pharaoh himself. (Genesis 40) Two years later he was invited to interpret Pharaoh's disturbing dreams. (Genesis 41:1-36) The dreams themselves were prophecies of coming abundance to be followed by years of terrible famine and Joseph, after interpreting the dreams, proposed a radical solution which greatly impressed Pharaoh and his court. In fact, they were so impressed that Joseph was immediately freed from prison and installed as the second in command of Pharaoh so that he could implement his plan. Here is the account:

> This proposal pleased Pharaoh and all his servants. And Pharaoh said to his servants, can we find a man like this, in whom is the Spirit of God? Then Pharaoh said to Joseph, Since God has shown you all this, there is none so discerning and wise as you are. You

shall be over my house, and all my people shall order themselves as you command. Only as regards the throne will I be greater than you. And Pharaoh said to Joseph, See, I have set you over all the land of Egypt. (Genesis 41:37-41)

And Joseph, the second in command (a.k.a. "2IC") executed his planned intervention so well that over the next 14 plus years two amazing things happened. First, Egypt survived the famine and Pharaoh thrived, emerging as the absolute owner of virtually all things in the land, including the people. Not a bad day's work! Second, and even more important, Joseph's brothers and their families eventually moved to Egypt to escape the ravages of the famine in Canaan, came under the protection of the boy they had betrayed now turned powerful and as a result the very nation of Israel was saved--and from that nation came our Savior, the Lord Jesus Christ!

What We Learn from Joseph

The story of Joseph is a great story. It is filled with intrigue and drama. It's a tale about a young man who emerges from tragedy to triumph--a plot we all love. And throughout the story we see two threads woven into its fabric. One thread is that of Joseph's abilities and impressive mind. The other is that of God's amazing, sovereign grace. In particular, I want us to explore three lessons from Joseph's life:

1. Joseph's life was all part of a grand, divine plan.

2. Joseph's life was what it was because it was accompanied by divine blessing.

3. Joseph's circumstances were filled with unfairness and injustice yet controlled by divine providence.

4. Joseph's impact came through creativity based on divine inspiration.

CHAPTER 8

LESSON ONE: JOSEPH'S LIFE WAS PART OF A GRAND, DIVINE PLAN

You don't have to be a Calvinist to believe that God is sovereign. The truth that God is in control of all things from before time, in time and beyond time is crystal clear in Scripture. We are not fatalists. We are not automatons. But we are creatures of the sovereign Creator and He does in our lives and in our world and in our circumstances exactly as He desires! Paul puts it this way in Ephesians: "In him we have obtained an inheritance, having been predestined according to the purpose of him who works all things according to the counsel of his will…" (Ephesians 1:11, ESV) Thankfully, our sovereign God is also infinitely kind and loving. Consider the well-known verse from Romans 8: "And we know that for those who love God all things work together for good, for those who are called according to his purpose." (Romans 8:28)

Clearly, Joseph believed this. Consider his words to his brothers when they were certain he would kill them.

When Joseph's brothers saw that their father was dead, they said, "It may be that Joseph will hate us and pay us back for all the evil that we did to him." So they sent a message to Joseph, saying, "Your father gave this command before he died: 'Say to Joseph, "Please forgive the transgression of your brothers and their sin, because they did evil to you."' And now, please forgive the transgression of the servants of the God of your father." Joseph wept when they spoke to him. His brothers also came and fell down before him and said, "Behold, we are your servants." But Joseph said to them, "Do not fear, for am I in the place of God? As for you, you meant evil against me, but God meant it for good, to bring it about that many people[b] should be kept alive, as they are today. So do not fear; I will provide for you and your little ones." Thus he comforted them and spoke kindly to them. (Genesis 50:15-21, ESV, italics mine)

Joseph understood, at least in his mature years, that his entire life had been part of a divine plan.

The Mystery of Providence

"Providence" is a word that does not appear in Scripture. Neither does "Trinity" for that matter. Yet both are tremendously important doctrines.

The Westminster Confession of Faith (the doctrinal summary of many reformed Christians) explains providence this way in the Shorter Catechism:

> Q. 11. What are God's works of providence?
> A. God's works of providence are his most holy, wise and powerful preserving and governing all his creatures, and all their actions.

As you consider this definition consider this also. The purpose of the Shorter Catechism is to teach children the basics of Christianity.

There are hundreds of books, papers and

other materials devoted to exploring this divine mystery. It's certainly not my purpose to add to that number. I simply recognize from Scripture that the hand of our God is active in our affairs, that He controls our circumstances, that there is no such thing as luck--good or bad, and that chaos or complexity theory is a great way of looking at life they only make sense when, behind them, we see God.

Another perspective on providence is to acknowledge that God has a plan--His plan--and that He has been, is and will be directly involved in seeing that plan realized in every detail. This is clearly evident in Joseph's life. Think through the events of our story:

- Conspired against by his brothers
- Near death but instead preserved
- Sold into slavery but rising to prominence
- Cast into prison yet trusted by the warden
- Introduced to Pharaoh
- Elevated to second in command
- Used by God to save Egypt and Israel

That didn't just happen. God's plan included all of this and, as with all things God planned, it came to pass.

The Preservation of God's People

From before time it was God's intention to create man and to redeem us from our fallenness, guilt and shame. Moreover, it was always to be done through the substitutionary atonement of His Only Son, our Lord Jesus Christ. This was no afterthought. This was His plan from the beginning. For Jesus to come into the world as a human being required a lineage; by God's choice this would be the lineage of Abraham (Genesis 12:1-3; Galatians 3:16). If Abraham's line was destroyed then the Messiah could not come (I speak in human terms!). This simple fact explains why the Enemy has been so intent on destroying Israel over the centuries. The threats to Israel's existence and God's consistent preservation of at least a remnant of Abraham's offspring is pretty much the story of the Old Testament in a nutshell. It is in this context that providence begins to make sense to us. God is sovereignly ensuring that His plan, in all of it's intricacy, is fulfilled.

In this particular story, Joseph is a key part

of this plan. Israel, an infant "nation" is threatened by an extreme famine. Yet, years before, God providentially arranged for a member of that nation to end up in Egypt. God providentially arranged for him to serve in a great house, to end up in prison, and to brought before the king where he predicted the famine and its solution. And then the famine struck--both Egypt and Israel; indeed, it struck the entire world. (Genesis 41: 53-56) Through Joseph's ideas food enough for Egypt and beyond was stored. The nations came to Egypt for this food and one of those nations was Israel. They were saved by this series of events and the lineage of Abraham continued. Joseph explains this to his brothers on more than one occasion

> And God sent me before you to preserve for you a remnant on earth, and to keep alive for you many survivors. So it was not you who sent me here, but God. He has made me a father to Pharaoh, and lord of all his house and ruler over all the land of Egypt. Hurry and go up to my father and say to him, 'Thus says your son Joseph, God has made me lord of all Egypt. Come down to me; do not

tarry. 10 You shall dwell in the land of Goshen, and you shall be near me, you and your children and your children's children, and your flocks, your herds, and all that you have. There I will provide for you, for there are yet five years of famine to come, so that you and your household, and all that you have, do not come to poverty.' And now your eyes see, and the eyes of my brother Benjamin see, that it is my mouth that speaks to you. (Genesis 45:7-12, ESV)

But Joseph said to them, "Do not fear, for am I in the place of God? As for you, you meant evil against me, but God meant it for good, to bring it about that many people should be kept alive, as they are today. (Genesis 50:19-20, ESV, italics mine)

God still has a plan--the same one from the beginning. He is bringing the peoples of earth to Himself and turning rebels in to worshippers from every kindred, tongue, tribe and nation (Revelation 7:9). You and I are a part of that plan every bit as much as Joseph.

The Divine Drama

Business people, especially those of us who are not in charge, often feel left out of the divine drama. God's plan is unfolding globally with beautiful results and we are, at best either spectators and/or financiers. Missionaries and pastors have the lead roles. Occasional business leaders and entrepreneurs get a speaking part. The rest of us, sadly, feel consigned to the seats or backstage. We don't really have a part.

Wrong! Joseph was not a missionary and he was not a pastor. He was a slave turned government employee and he was a vital part of the plan of God, the great divine drama of redemption. So are you! None of us exists by accident. We are not in our current roles by chance. You and I are in business (or whatever calling we may be in) by the sovereign design of God, the providential God. We have a part to play. Global missions and the discipling of the nations is not limited to the "professionals" or the "super spiritual." It is for everybody. It is for you.

Your part and mine may be small in our eyes. I kind of hope they are so we don't fall prey to the devil's snare of pride and hubris. However, if in the divine plan of God not even a bird can fall from the sky without the Father taking notice (Luke 12:6-7) how much more does your life matter? It matters more than you can imagine. Your part will not be played by another. It will be played by you and your life will have exactly the impact on the great outcome that God originally intended.

Here's a fun truth. When it comes to God's cosmic drama, the amazing plot, we have both inconspicuous parts and vital parts. On the one hand we are just walk owns; Joseph was a walk on. He was there by grace as much as we are and not because he was a supremely talented person. On the other hand, we are critical. Had Joseph not done the things he did and had God not engineered Joseph's circumstances the way He did Abraham's seed would not have been delivered in the way it was.

Conclusion

Can I throw you a lifeline right about now? We are walking on a narrow ledge when it comes to trying to explain or understand the sovereignty of God. There are always the slopes of total fatalistic "nothing matters" approaches and there are the "it's really all on my shoulders" fallacy. Balance is not the answer though it is the popular solution. On balance, one foot in boiling water and one in ice water is comfortable but somehow that doesn't work. In the same way weakening divine sovereignty or human responsibility so that we can "fit them together" is a pretty unsatisfying doctrine. Can we agree that the Bible teaches that God is in control and that we are responsible for our actions? And can we further agree that, like the Trinity, nobody actually understands it? Great!

Now we can get back to our point. The first lesson from Joseph is a wonderful truth for all of us. Our lives, our calling, our jobs, our roles as "not in charge," are all part of an incredibly grand, divine plan. That makes our work, our workplace, our shop, our office incredibly grand as well! I don't have to leave my job or be the CEO to be significant. I don't have to sell my company and go into "ministry" to be meaningful. I am. You are. We are!

CHAPTER 9

LESSON TWO: JOSEPH'S LIFE WAS ACCOMPANIED BY DIVINE BLESSING

One of the mantras we constantly hear in the business world is, "You can do it!" Another is "Together we can!" Premised on the flawed view that man is capable of great things on his own, self help gurus have proliferated this nonsense globally. Believers in the marketplace find themselves drowning in this kind of "positive thinking" and pretty soon start believing it; after all, it's hard to hear God's truth an hour or two a week and the world's "truth" the other 50 or 60 hours and keep our heads straight.

In the hands of today's motivational speakers and writers and bloggers and tweeters, Joseph's story would be dramatized into a "young man overcomes tremendous adversity to become powerful man by grit and determination" message. He did it. So can you.

However, throughout Joseph's rise to impact and kingdom influence we see a consistent message: Joseph's life was blessed by God. Clearly he was a remarkable man. Anyone can see that. However, it is not his remarkable talents or intellect that are the reason for what happened in his life. It was the free, gracious blessing of God.

If you and I are attacking the day--in the general pursuit of business impact as well as in the headlong pursuit of Kingdom Impact--we will not be well prepared if our belief is that we can do it, that we are up to it, that our education or motivation or situation are the keys to our success. We would do well to be regularly reminded of two truths that are as real in the workplace as they are in the worship place:

> I am the vine; you are the branches. Whoever abides in me and I in him, he it is that bears much fruit, for apart from me you can do nothing. (John 15:5, ESV, italics mine)

> I can do all things through him who strengthens me. (Philippians 4:13, ESV, italics mine)

Beware of thinking that our dependence upon Christ is limited to the church or to other forms of "ministry." As the old Puritans used to say, "Even our hearts stop between beats to ask, 'Again, Lord?'"

Joseph in Potiphar's House

Now Joseph had been brought down to Egypt, and Potiphar, an officer of Pharaoh, the captain of the guard, an Egyptian, had bought him from the Ishmaelites who had brought him down there. The LORD was with Joseph, and he became a successful man, and he was in the house of his Egyptian master. His master saw that the LORD was with him and that the LORD caused all that he did to succeed in his hands. So Joseph found favor in his sight and attended him, and he made him overseer of his house and put him in charge of all that he had. From the time that he made him overseer in his house and over all that he had, the LORD blessed the Egyptian's house for Joseph's sake; the blessing of the LORD was on all that he had, in house and field. So he left all that he had in Joseph's charge, and because of him he had no concern about anything but the food he ate. (Genesis 39:1-6, ESV, italics mine)

This is an amazing account. Joseph was sold as a slave, transported to a foreign land and essentially serving in bondage in the household of Potiphar. Yet it is here that we read that "the Lord was with him." How many of us would acknowledge that the Lord was with us when things are definitely not going our way?

Four things jump out of this passage at us in addition to the fact that the God was, in fact, with Joseph. There are four critically important outcomes of God's presence and faithfulness.

First, Joseph became successful. (Genesis 39:2-3) Joseph's success was the result of God's blessing and grace. I'm sure he worked hard. I'm sure he was smart. I'm sure that he did all the things a good slave would do. But the Bible attributes his success in this setting to the hand of God. It is hard, I know, to think this way but it is the way we must think. Whatever success you and I have experienced is due to the involvement of God and not something we should claim for ourselves. Like Joseph we work hard, we try hard, we do the right things. And, like Joseph, if we succeed we need to stop and realize, "I didn't get here alone. God is with me." And, just to keep things in some kind of Scriptural balance, when we are in the hard places of failure and frustration God is with us there also!

Second, Potiphar realized that Joseph was God's man. (Genesis 39:3) When unbelievers or weak believers see success they attribute it to the man. But somehow Potiphar understood that Joseph's abilities stemmed from God. And not just any "god." Potiphar saw that YAHWEH, the true God of the Hebrews, was the source of Joseph's strength. What a thing to pray for. "Lord, grant that men may see Your hand in my life at work and attribute it to You, the one true God and not to some vague 'god' or 'karma' or 'the universe!'"

Third, God's blessing led to Joseph's promotion. It is a kingdom principle that faithfulness over little leads to responsibility over much. Soon, Joseph moves from being an ordinary house slave to being the overseer of the entire business, second only to Potiphar himself. (Genesis 39:4.6. ESV) I cannot guarantee that God's blessing on your work will lead to your career advancement but it's more likely it will than it won't!

Fourth, God's grace and prospering of Joseph spilled over to the business he managed as well. (Genesis 39:5) Many years ago I was asked by one of my clients to come in and lead a divisional turnaround. They were prepared to close the division but wanted to give it one last shot. To make a long story short, within three years not only was the division growing but we had actually become larger than all the other divisions of the company combined. This was during the same period in which God was calling me to be involved in kingdom business startups in Central Asia. My assessment of what happened is well expressed in Joseph's story. The blessing of God on my life by His grace spilled over to bless the company I worked for at the same time.

Joseph in Prison

You will remember that in spite of his blessed success in Potiphar's employ Joseph was falsely accused by Potiphar's wanton wife and consigned to prison. Here's the account:

> And Joseph's master took him and put him into the prison, the place where the king's prisoners were confined,

and he was there in prison. But the LORD was with Joseph and showed him steadfast love and gave him favor in the sight of the keeper of the prison. And the keeper of the prison put Joseph in charge of all the prisoners who were in the prison. Whatever was done there, he was the one who did it. The keeper of the prison paid no attention to anything that was in Joseph's charge, because the LORD was with him. And whatever he did, the LORD made it succeed. (Genesis 39:20-223, ESV, italics mine)

Second verse same as the first. Joseph, in spite of being imprisoned for something he didn't do, never lost the presence or blessing of God. As before, God prospered Joseph. He caused his work to succeed. He gave him favor in the sight of the warden.

In a parallel experience, shortly after we completed the turnaround of the failing division mentioned above, I was asked to leave. Naive to corporate politics I was too trusting (I still am) and paid the price. However, within 3 days of leaving I had formed a new company that went on to work globally and became an example of what a true Kingdom Company could be and a base for much Business as Mission work around the world. Why? Because the grace of God and the blessing of God was still with me.

By way of application I have to remind us all that the blessing of God on our lives is part of a much bigger whole than just our career. It is not just a steadily upward moving trajectory. It may involve great success and great failure. Remember, God is executing a grand plan and we are only a part of it. Nevertheless, we are blessed and, regardless of our circumstances, we can trust that the hand of God has not departed from our lives and that He will honor Himself and fulfill His purposes...period!

Joseph in Pharaoh's Court

Through a series of events that can only explained by divine providence, Joseph goes from prison to appear before Pharaoh as an interpreter of dreams. (Genesis 40-41:36) Perhaps you wonder at times how you go to where you are. The answer is God. Rest in that.

Here in this exalted setting where, no doubt, Joseph was surrounded by the brightest minds of

Egypt and other lands, the blessing of God on his life is clear to all--even the king. After Joseph interprets Pharaoh's dreams and uses them to advise Pharaoh on the best strategy to address the predicted famine, the king expresses his amazement:

> And Pharaoh said to his servants, "Can we find a man like this, in whom is the Spirit of God?" Then Pharaoh said to Joseph, "Since God has shown you all this, there is none so discerning and wise as you are. You shall be over my house, and all my people shall order themselves as you command. Only as regards the throne will I be greater than you." (Genesis 41:37-40, ESV)

The pattern is clear. Grace precedes and enables all else. God's blessing rest on men of His choosing because of love not merit. The hand of God leads to success (and at times failure) and never leaves us. Advancement is often the result and goodness to the company for which we work. In the end, God receives the glory and we receive the joy.

Conclusion

This second lesson from Joseph is truly important. Whether you are an entrepreneur, a CEO, an executive or an entry level employee God is with you. If you are His then He is with you. Learn to see Him at work. Learn to see Him in work. Learn to rely upon Him more than yourself and watch what happens--even in jail!

CHAPTER 10

LESSON THREE: JOSEPH'S CIRCUMSTANCES WERE FILLED WITH UNFAIRNESS YET CONTROLLED BY DIVINE PROVIDENCE

If you have children or grandchildren you are not unfamiliar with the constant, "That's not fair!" complaint. Humans, as a species, seem to have a basic operating system that demands that everything be fair, equal, and equitable.

But life is not fair. It is not equal. It is not equitable. Injustice abounds. Good guys don't always win and cheaters do prosper--at least for a while (Psalm 73). Nowhere is this more profoundly realized than in business. Whether you are the founder, the investor, the executive, the assistant or a temporary employee there is one thing you can count on: unfair things will happen in your life.

Joseph certainly had his share of unfairness in his life. Yet, for all the unfair and unjust treatment at the hands of men, these circumstances were still under the control of God.

Unjustly Sold into Slavery

We have already looked at the story in Genesis 37. Joseph was unfairly his father's favorite; this, in turn, led to jealousy on the part of his brothers--again unfair for how can you blame Joseph for Jacob's failure as a parent? (Genesis 37:4) Joseph's brothers then plotted to kill him and, by the hand of God, ended up selling him to a passing slave caravan instead. (Genesis 37:12-28)

There is a powerful memoir written by Solomon Northrup entitled Twelve Years a Slave. [2] Northrup, born a free man in the north, was kidnapped and sold into slavery in the pre-Civil War south. For 12 years Northrup's lead character labored and suffered as chattel. He witnessed and experienced the cruel treatment of slave owners and overseers. Finally, through the help of one white man his friends from Massachusetts found him and returned him to his family. Unfair? Without question.

Unjustly Imprisoned

Was Joseph to blame for being attractive to Potiphar's immoral wife? Was he to blame for her

---

[2] Northrup, Solomon. *Twelve Years a Slave.* (Dover Publications, 2000)

advances? Her arrogance and dishonesty? Of course not. But it didn't matter. As soon as Potiphar heard his wife's accusations he had Joseph cast into prison where, presumably, he would die. (Genesis 39:7-20)

Life is like that. Innocent people go to jail all the time. True followers of Jesus go to jail all over the world. On a much smaller scale, people are passed over for promotion, cheated out of stock options, unpaid for contracts fulfilled and experience many more unfair things.

Unjustly Forgotten

In prison Joseph became a trusted assistant to the warden. (Genesis 39:21-23) He was given the opportunity to interpret dreams for two of Pharaoh's servants--his baker and his cupbearer. One dream turned out to be a prediction of death for the baker and came true; the other was a prediction of restoration to Pharaoh's service for the cupbearer and also came true. (Genesis 40:1-22)

Predictably, if you are thinking through the story, Joseph requested that these servants remember what he had done for them and help get him out of the prison. Obviously the baker ended up no help but to the cupbearer Joseph said:

> In three days Pharaoh will lift up your head and restore you to your office, and you shall place Pharaoh's cup in his hand as formerly, when you were his cupbearer. Only remember me, when it is well with you, and please do me the kindness to mention me to Pharaoh, and so get me out of this house. For I was indeed stolen out of the land of the Hebrews, and here also I have done nothing that they should put me into the pit. (Genesis 40:13-15)

Did the cupbearer help? No. He promptly forgot. "Yet the chief cupbearer did not remember Joseph, but forgot him." (Genesis 40:23) Ungrateful. Unfair.

Sound familiar? "Sure," says your co-worker. "I'll make sure the boss knows you were a big part of this success." Right!

Conclusion

"Life is hard and then you die." These were words often spoken to us at seminary by one particularly pessimistic church history professor. But, for all his pessimism, he was at least partly right. Life is hard. Life is unjust.

What is true in general is magnified in the business community--globally. It doesn't matter whether you are vying for a senior position on Wall Street, a new lease on Main Street or a business license in an unnamed street in some 4th world country. When there is money and power involved injustice intensifies, dishonesty is common, cheating and corruption grows. It's now wonder that many people (wrongly) attribute an inherent evil to business. Of course, it's not business it's the people in business in the same way that it's not the church or the government or the school or any other institution; it's people. As Jeremiah correctly observed, "The heart is deceitful above all things, and desperately sick; who can understand it?" (Jeremiah 17:9, ESV)

The Christian in business, the disciple who is called to live in and pursue Business as Mission will do well to remember the consistent unfairness with which Joseph was treated--even by his own family! We would also do well to remember that in each circumstance, as grossly unjust as it may have been, the Lord was with Joseph and in total control of everything. (Genesis 39:2, 21; 41:38; 45:9; 50:20) We will be treated unfairly. I guarantee it. Yet God is always with us. He will never leave us, fail us, or forsake us. There is rest in the battle in that reality!

CHAPTER 11

LESSON FOUR: JOSEPH'S IMPACT CAME THROUGH CREATIVITY THAT WAS DIVINELY INSPIRED

Many years ago I heard the story of Japanese factory worker who was trying to deal with a piece of equipment that was malfunctioning. He tried everything he knew but with no success. To make matters worse, senior management and guests from Germany were touring the facility. They came to the machine operator's area. As you can imagine, the worker was greatly embarrassed but before he could say anything the Holy Spirit spoke to him. "Kneel down and pray," He said. Several times, much to the consternation of the employee, the Spirit said the same thing. Reluctantly, he obeyed and, as the managers and their guests looked on, he knelt to pray...only to look ahead and this new, lower angle and see what the problem was. He immediately fixed the machine to the applause and approval of the observers. Strange? Maybe. Again, maybe not.

Joseph endured much prosperity and degradation all the while being blessed by his sovereign and ever-present God. Now, it's time for his big impact, his breakthrough. And it came to him in just such a miraculous way.

His First Break

In Hollywood we often hear about the movie role that was some star's "first break." In business we hear the same thing. Some project, some introduction, some networking connection, some classmate--something opens a door that leads to other doors that lead to success.

Joseph's first break came, of all places, in prison. Genesis 40 is the account of Joseph and Pharaoh's two servants. From a human perspective this is the classic "chance encounter." We know better, of course. God arranged every detail for this moment when Joseph would be asked to interpret dreams that the two men had-- one of death and one of restoration. Even though the cupbearer forgot Joseph initially it was this event that opened the door to another, a door of world changing impact.

In my own life I attribute much of what I am involved in today and the impact of global BAM work to just such a chance meeting. I was teaching a leadership workshop in the late 1980's for a client who had, by God's hand, invited guests from their largest client. One of the guests came up to me at a break and observed, "You are a Christian, aren't you?" The ensuing conversation and friendship was the plan of God to eventually introduce me to Kyrgyzstan a few years later and that providential introduction changed everything!

Never despise the day of small things! Be open to the connections God makes for you and for the opportunities He ordains. You may not recognize them at the moment but they are all of divine origin.

His Second Break

It was two years after this first break that the cupbearer, now restored to Pharaoh's service, remembered Joseph. Here's the account following Pharaoh's complaint of troubling dreams and the inability of his wise men to interpret them:

> Then the chief cupbearer said to Pharaoh, "I remember my offenses today. When Pharaoh was angry with his servants and put me and the chief

baker in custody in the house of the captain of the guard, we dreamed on the same night, he and I, each having a dream with its own interpretation. A young Hebrew was there with us, a servant of the captain of the guard. When we told him, he interpreted our dreams to us, giving an interpretation to each man according to his dream. And as he interpreted to us, so it came about. I was restored to my office, and the baker was hanged." Then Pharaoh sent and called Joseph, and they quickly brought him out of the pit. And when he had shaved himself and changed his clothes, he came in before Pharaoh. (Genesis 41:9-14, ESV)

Once again by divine orchestration Joseph gets a break. This time it is not a prison encounter but a royal audience. In the perfect timing that only God has the cupbearer remembers Joseph and he is quickly invited to meet with Pharaoh.

The company I am with now (and have worked with as a consultant turned employee for 17 years) is led by a man to whom I was introduced to over lunch back in 1997. An innocuous discussion of workers' compensation issues, of all things, was the beginning of a relationship that has set the stage for this book.

His Big Break

As Joseph listened to Pharaoh's dreams of cows--skinny and healthy--God gave the interpretation to Joseph. Joseph recognized this and made it clear that his insight was from God:

> Joseph answered Pharaoh, "It is not in me; God will give Pharaoh a favorable answer." (Genesis 41:16, ESV)

> Then Joseph said to Pharaoh, "The dreams of Pharaoh are one; God has revealed to Pharaoh what he is about to do..." (Genesis 41:25, ESV)

It is exciting to see God's hand in the open. Up until this point in Joseph's life we have mostly seen providence in action. Now, as in the prison encounter, it is the supernatural intervention of God that moves Joseph into prominence. God gives Joseph an amazing insight, an inspired insight.

Have you ever had that happen in your career? Why should we be surprised in business that, when we pray for wisdom and grace for our employer, our company, and our co-workers that God actually grants it?

At one company in which I worked for a few years I was asked by the Chairman of the Board, "If I gave you $500,000 what would you do to grow your division?" Without hesitation or premeditation I answered with something I had never thought of before. He told me to get on with it and, as a result, we launched a new product that changed the face of our entire industry!

Another such intervention of God occurred while we were launching a cluster of small businesses in the North Caucasus region of Russia. One business development team, comprised of an interpreter, a US coach and a local entrepreneur, was working on launching a cattle ranch. As they wrestled with the business plan and the financial modeling they simply could not make it work. Frustrated to the point of tears, the team decided to call it a day and pray for a solution. That night the coach had a dream in which he believed God gave him the answer to the problem. The entrepreneur had exactly the same dream. Both were hyper-anxious to meet the next day and share what God had shown them. Imagine their astonishment when they recounted the exact same dream to each other! Even more, when they plugged the numbers into the plan it worked perfectly--some would say divinely!

No one will ever convince me that God doesn't inspire business ideas and solutions! Inspiration is not limited to entrepreneurs, though. It often comes to the rest of us, solves business challenges, launches new products and services, and provides a great opportunity for witness.

His Inspired Business Plan

So what actually happened? God not only provided Joseph with the interpretation of Pharaoh's dream--7 years of plenty followed by 7 years of extreme famine. God also gave Joseph the creative solution:

> It is as I told Pharaoh; God has shown to Pharaoh what he is about to do. There will come seven years of great

plenty throughout all the land of Egypt, but after them there will arise seven years of famine, and all the plenty will be forgotten in the land of Egypt. The famine will consume the land, and the plenty will be unknown in the land by reason of the famine that will follow, for it will be very severe. And the doubling of Pharaoh's dream means that the thing is fixed by God, and God will shortly bring it about. Now therefore let Pharaoh select a discerning and wise man, and set him over the land of Egypt. Let Pharaoh proceed to appoint overseers over the land and take one-fifth of the produce of the land[b] of Egypt during the seven plentiful years. And let them gather all the food of these good years that are coming and store up grain under the authority of Pharaoh for food in the cities, and let them keep it. That food shall be a reserve for the land against the seven years of famine that are to occur in the land of Egypt, so that the land may not perish through the famine." (Genesis 41:28-36, ESV)

Consequently, Pharaoh was so impressed that, as we have seen, he immediately promoted Joseph to the "second in command" position over all of Egypt so that he could implement his plan.

His Implementation

Joseph set about to do just what he had outlined and, as a result, launched a series of business ventures that are the forerunners of modern industries, enriched his chief shareholder, and saved Egypt (as well as Israel). Here's a summary of his innovations:

1. Commodities Trading (Genesis 41:33-36)

    Joseph determined that not only did they need to store grain they also needed to trade in it. He established a management structure and began to collect grain during the prosperous times that he would later used to acquire great wealth and property for Pharaoh.

2. Capital Accumulation (Genesis 41:53-57; 47:14)

Read the story:

> So when the famine had spread over all the land, Joseph opened all the storehouses[h]and sold to the Egyptians, for the famine was severe in the land of Egypt. Moreover, all the earth came to Egypt to Joseph to buy grain, because the famine was severe over all the earth. (Genesis 41:56-57, ESV)

Joseph managed to create a "global market" for much needed food. His international trading of product for cash made Pharaoh even richer than he had been before.

> And Joseph gathered up all the money that was found in the land of Egypt and in the land of Canaan, in exchange for the grain that they bought. And Joseph brought the money into

Pharaoh's house. (Genesis 47:14, ESV)

3.   Livestock Acquisition (Genesis 47:15-17)

It wasn't long before the severe famine that Joseph had predicted required the people to once again purchase grain from Pharaoh's storehouse. This time, having run out of money they traded their cattle, horses, and other animals for their food.

4.   Investment in Real Estate (Genesis 47:18-20)

It seems that real estate has always been a good business to be in--with a few atypical exceptions. This period was not one of those:

And when that year was ended, they came to him the following year and said to him, "We will not hide from my lord that our money is all spent. The herds of livestock are my lord's. There is nothing left in the sight of my lord but our bodies and our land. Why should we die before your eyes, both we and our land? Buy us and our land for food, and we with our land will be servants to Pharaoh. And give us seed that we may live and not die, and that the land may not be desolate." So Joseph bought all the land of Egypt for Pharaoh, for all the Egyptians sold their fields, because the famine was severe on them. The land became Pharaoh's. As for the people, he made servants of them from one end of Egypt to the other. (Genesis 47:18-21)

Again, in desperation the people who had not planned sold their property and became servants (essentially employees) in order to procure food.

5. Ongoing Revenue (Genesis 47:23-26)

Some want to call this a Fair Tax scheme! Any business that relies on significant, one time transactions is in trouble once those transactions are consummated. Having acquired money, livestock, land and employees/servant, Joseph wisely (divine wisdom as we know) launched a sustainable business model.

The famine would end. Commerce would recover. Recessions don't last forever. So, Joseph set about to help the people restart their own farming and, at the same time, set in place a production sharing program that was both fair and wealth generating for his boss.

His Pure Motives

One last point remains to be made from Joseph's amazing and inspired business program: his heart. Gordon Gecko, the fictitious caricature of Wall Street investing, famously declared, "Greed is good!" in the movie Wall Street. Unfortunately, while some people in fact subscribe to this selfish approach to business, most employees and business owners aren't really "in it just for the money." In my career, both as executive coach, strategic advisor and now senior executive I've rarely met anyone like Gecko. What I do find is people who want to make a difference, who want to help people, to create product, to offer services, and, yes, to make money.

Joseph is a prime example of business person, a second in command, who had good motives. His original motivation was to feed the people and to save the land (Genesis 41:36). Even after creating enormous wealth for Pharaoh Joseph's heart remained with the people and that is why he gave them "seed grants" to reestablish themselves (Genesis 47:23).

Two cautions here. First, don't let people, especially other Christians, look down on you or suspiciously at you because you are in business or because you sell things or because you bring value to your shareholders and company leaders. Your profession is an honorable one. Second, be constantly in touch with your heart. There is a Gordon Gecko in all of us; it is the work of the Holy Spirit in sanctification to purify our motives and enable us to do what we do for the right reasons!

Conclusion

So we see that God Himself can and does give creative ideas and solutions to business leaders. What a blessing it must have been to Pharaoh to have a man like Joseph on his team. I wonder if we are that kind of blessing to our companies?

CHAPTER 12

REVIEWING OUR HEROES

Originally this book was going to be entitled The Daniel Factor. This was because I was taken with Daniel's impact as a "second in command." Then I rediscovered Joseph and his impact as a "not the boss." Both are huge encouragements to me and, by now, I hope to you, in our respective roles in business.

For the sake of retention and application let's review the 7 key lessons from their lives:

1. Daniel's place was God's place for him. So is yours. Embrace it.

2. Daniel's life demonstrated the authenticity of his faith. Live it.

3. Daniel's words pointed men to God. Speak them.

4. Joseph's place was part of a grand, divine plan. Yours and mine as well. Play it.

5. Joseph's life was accompanied and made successful by divine blessing. Look for it.

6. Joseph's circumstances were filled with unfairness that was still controlled by divine providence. Rest in it.

7. Joseph's impact came through creativity based on divine inspiration. Risk it.

Now the balance of this book will address specific challenges, resources and practices that every 2IC understands all too well.

CHAPTER 13

SPIRITUAL AUTHORITY IN THE MARKETPLACE

There are so many books on leadership out there that I hesitate to even go close to the subject. However, there is one question related to leadership that constantly nags at me as I discuss business as mission with practitioners around the world. It is this: why is that while in the church followers of Jesus feel confident while in the marketplace we feel powerless, out of place and ineffective?

I've identified three major types of leadership and authority that we need to explore. The differences between them are crucial. For the purpose of this book I am using the terms leadership, authority and power interchangeably; that is how we use them in real life and not in the rarified atmosphere of theoretical discussions.

First, there is positional authority, i.e. the power that flows from virtue of my place in the org chart. I am a vice president so I have authority over a director but subordinate to a senior vice president. I have a "C" in front of my title consequently I have more corporate power than a manager. We are all used to this concept. It is the food chain, the pecking order, the power structure or whatever else people call it. To be sure, positional authority is real; however, I would suggest that if you have to use it you've already failed in the big picture. Positional authority actually weakens as you wield it.

Second, there is influential authority. All of the current speakers and writers on the topic of leadership are pushing this type of power. And I agree with them. On the purely horizontal or human level. When it comes to moving people into action influence is far better than position. As we used to say in the days when I led a franchise operation, "If you have to pull out the contract to get a franchisee to do something you've lost even if you win." When you make people do things or coerce them by virtue of position or legal standing then they may do what you require but the relationship is forever damaged. By contrast, when I can influence someone to act or to move in a certain direction based on open communication, trust, character and their belief that I have their best interest at heart and that I know what I'm talking about that kind of authority grows with exercise. Character and competence are a true and beneficial form of power.

Third, there is spiritual authority. This is kingdom authority. It is the authority of the Spirit. It has nothing to do with position. It is connected to influence since character is a kingdom virtue. Yet it is distinct and infinitely more efficacious. This is the kind of authority I want to walk in as a follower of Jesus. This is the kind of authority exercised by prophets and apostles. This is the kind of power exercised by a CEO and an entry level employee alike. This is the kind of leadership that transcends all barriers and boundaries. It is as meaningful in the corporate boardroom as it is in church or the Asian factory or the African hospital or the Central American coffee warehouse.

Over the years many of us have spent hours thinking about and teaching on Jesus' explanation of leadership as a servant function. Here is the text. It follows a request on the part of the mother of James and John that her sons be granted position in Jesus' kingdom; His reply is astounding:

> But Jesus called them to him and said, "You know that the rulers of the Gentiles lord it over them, and their

great ones exercise authority over them. It shall not be so among you. But whoever would be great among you must be your servant, and whoever would be first among you must be your slave, even as the Son of Man came not to be served but to serve, and to give his life as a ransom for many." (Matthew 20:25-28, ESV)

Now most of us are quick to conclude that the point that Jesus is making here is that the style and motivation of Christian leadership should be different than that of pagans. And, of course, it should. The unbelieving Gentiles (no doubt He was thinking of the Roman rulers of Israel at the time) appear, as a lot, to have been selfish, domineering and demanding; Jesus' followers were not to act in such a manner but instead with the attitude and heart of servants. This interpretation is true as far as it goes.

However, I think there is another dimension here entirely. Note that Jesus equates "lord it over them" (the typical negative expression about leadership) with "exercise authority over them" (the typical positive expression). In other words, there is more here than just motivation and attitude. The problem with the Gentiles is that the primary type of leadership or authority or greatness they knew was essentially positional. Their paradigm of authority was about title. They had governmental or economic standing and therefore they had power.

In Jesus' kingdom authority flows from a different place altogether. What does the servant have? Not much. The main thing the servant has is actually based on what they don't have. They don't have positional authority; they are peons. They certainly may have a certain influence but it is unlikely to be very impactful. Mail room clerks and receptionists have little effect on their companies even when they have the greatest of character. A servant has a different kind of power. What a servant has available to them is spiritual authority. Jesus had it and He was a servant. We can have it as well as we take our position as servants like our Master!

So what makes up spiritual power? I suggest that, beyond the obvious answer of the fullness of the Holy Spirit, there are at least 5 keys to exercising spiritual authority and impact at work. I call them the Five I's; the disciple who embraces them will find God's power at work in their work.

1. Integration
2. Identity
3. Intentionality
4. Integrity
5. Imitation

Integration

One of the reasons that Christians in business have limited impact is that they often feel that they are on enemy territory, i.e. business is the devil's domain. We are there by necessity--we have to pay the bills, we have to have a visa, etc. With this faulty worldview in place it's now wonder we come to believe the lying whispers of the Deceiver, "You're out of place. You don't belong here."

We've already touched on this to a certain degree but let me say this as bluntly as I know how. There is no place on earth that is not God's place, no domain that is not God's domain. There is no sacred-secular divide. All of life is to be lived under the lordship of Jesus Christ and that makes all of life equally sacred and equally His.

Whether I am in the church building, at the

dinner table, on the mission field or in the shop, I am in God's place. It's my Father's house. Spiritual authority comes when we know that we are exactly where God wants us.

Identity

Here's another truth that will give you confidence in the world of commerce: you are God's man (or woman) in God's place.

There's a silly story from WWII that my old Australian mentor used to tell us when we were missionaries in training. During the war, a couple of Aussie privates were lost in London about half drunk on a typical foggy night. A young English officer walked by them and, to his astonishment, they ignored him and failed to salute. The officer quickly crossed the street, circled back and walked past them a second time. The Australians ignored him again. Frustrated he repeated his pass only to be ignored a third time. He burst out at the two men, "Don't you know who I am?" One of the soldiers turned to the other one and said, "Well, we thought we had it bad. We don't know where we are but this bloke doesn't know who he is!"

The problem is that in reality most Christians don't know who they are. We believe we are what we were: fallen sinners, weak and powerless. The truth is that, while still sinful and in desperate need of the grace of God, we are not what we once were. We are in Christ. We were in Adam by virtue of our natural birth and natural relation to him. We are now in Christ by virtue of our new birth and our supernatural relation to Him. This is one of the greatest truths in the entire New Testament and appears in various forms over 100 times.

In Adam, all that was true of Adam was true of us. Condemnation. Corruption. Failure. Rebels. Objects of wrath. Subjects of Satan. In Christ, all that is true of Jesus is true of us. Justification. Redemption. Sanctification. Freedom from the power of sin. Adoption as sons. Lavished in grace. Think deeply on these words from 2 Corinthians: "Therefore, if anyone is in Christ, he is a new creation. The old has passed away; behold, the new has come." (2 Corinthians 5:17 ESV)

When we walk into any setting, especially our place of employment, how do we think of ourselves? What is our identity? Do we see ourselves as fallen, out of place failures? Or do we see ourselves in Christ? Do we see ourselves as the servants of the Living God, children of the King, friends of Jesus, containers of the Holy Spirit? Spiritual authority is found in those who know they are found in Jesus!

Intentionality

I have written a great deal in my previous book, Business as Mission, about the principle of intentionality. For an entrepreneur or business owner it is about the deliberate connection of their business, their company to God's eternal purpose of redemption, restoration and transformation. The same principle applies to the employee, the 2IC, the "not the boss." Our job, our task, our career connects to what God is doing in the world too.

When I see work as "making the doughnuts" or "putting my nose to the grindstone" then I fail to understand just how strategic my job is. However, if I am connected and all that I am is connected to God's purpose intentionally then I walk with a confidence and sense of adventure that is hard to describe. Connected to and involved directly in discipling the nations and seeing Jesus honored and obeyed around the world from my office or sale counter makes everything different. I matter. My job matters. And there is spiritual authority in intentionality, in deliberate connectedness to God's work.

Integrity

One piece of God's armor that we are to don in our lives is the "breastplate of righteousness." (Ephesians 6:14) Many scholars identify this as holding our confidence in the imputed righteousness of Jesus. There is merit in that thought, pun intended. However, it makes more sense in context and in practical application if we see this as covering our hearts with integrity, with specific and active righteous living in contrast to deceit and disobedience.

Let me ask you this. When you know that you are indulging in sin, hidden and secret as it may be, do you sense the power of God? Are you confident wielding your spiritual authority? My guess is no. Certainly my own experience is no. Now I am not saying that your personal righteousness merits anything with God nor am I saying that spiritual authority relies on your performance. It is all of grace and all in Christ. However, the Scriptures are clear that, on the one hand, "if I regard iniquity in my heart He will not hear me" (Psalm 66:18). On the other hand, there is a powerful reality in our lives when we "walk in the light as He is in the light." (1 John 1:7)

My brothers and sisters guard your hearts and guard your integrity. Nothing will diffuse spiritual authority more quickly as a failure in this area.

Imitation

By imitation I mean simply that we need to learn to walk as Jesus walked, to live as Jesus lived, to fight as Jesus fought. "Therefore be imitators of God, as beloved children." (Ephesians 5:1 ESV) Historically, Christians have spent a lot of time thinking about how Jesus lived and seeking to emulate Him. In our day it seems that is considered some kind of fleshly striving. So consider these points.

How did Jesus discern what God wanted? Education or prayer? How did Jesus handle conflict? Clever words and humor or head on? How did Jesus fight the evil one? Effort or Scripture?

We have abandoned the proven tools and resources and weapons of our spiritual warfare. Instead we have learned to rely on strategy, marketing, cleverness, and other inadequate means. Remember it is spiritual authority we are discussing and spiritual authority requires spiritual means. As Paul declared:

> For though we walk in the flesh, we are not waging war according to the flesh. For the weapons of our warfare are not of the flesh but have divine power to destroy strongholds. We destroy arguments and every lofty opinion raised against the knowledge of God, and take every thought captive to obey Christ, being ready to punish every disobedience, when your obedience is complete. (2 Corinthians 10:3-6, ESV)

It is time that Christians realized that the armor of God (Ephesians 6: is not for use in the church and not restricted to direct missionary activity. It applies powerfully to any believer in any situation and none more vitally than the employee in business. Think of this passage the next time you prepare for work:

> Finally, be strong in the Lord and in the strength of his might. Put on the whole armor of God, that you may be

able to stand against the schemes of the devil. For we do not wrestle against flesh and blood, but against the rulers, against the authorities, against the cosmic powers over this present darkness, against the spiritual forces of evil in the heavenly places. Therefore take up the whole armor of God, that you may be able to withstand in the evil day, and having done all, to stand firm. Stand therefore, having fastened on the belt of truth, and having put on the breastplate of righteousness, and, as shoes for your feet, having put on the readiness given by the gospel of peace. In all circumstances take up the shield of faith, with which you can extinguish all the flaming darts of the evil one; and take the helmet of salvation, and the sword of the Spirit, which is the word of God, praying at all times in the Spirit, with all prayer and supplication. To that end keep alert with all perseverance, making supplication for all the saints, (Ephesians 6:10-18 ESV)

Conclusion

As believers we are meant to make an impact. Again, I remind you that it's not just at church. It's in business and it's everywhere. Some of you reading this book are working in your home country as employees. Some are working in businesses that are purposefully BAM but you are not in charge. Some of you are in between. It doesn't matter. In all settings we need to walk in spiritual authority--in the power and confidence that is ours in Christ!

CHAPTER 14

CHALLENGES AND DANGERS FOR THE 2IC

Daniel had his Lion's Den, political enemies and spiritual resistance to his prayers. Joseph had betrayal after betrayal. You will too. As my old mentor used to say, "Forward into battle." His point was that if you are serious about serving Jesus and seeing His kingdom expanded and people come to know Him in any location and in any culture you will face opposition, challenge and difficulty. The path is fraught with danger. This chapter will identify some of the more common dangers and offer suggestions for avoiding or overcoming each of them.

Pleasing to Whom?

Everyone of us knows the constant challenge in trying to remain faithful to Christ and focused on serving Him in and through business. Keeping our minds clear that we are not ultimately working for men but for men as unto the Lord is just plain hard. We know the admonition of Paul:

Bondservants, obey your earthly

masters with fear and trembling, with
a sincere heart, as you would Christ,
not by the way of eye-service, as
people-pleasers, but as bondservants
of Christ, doing the will of God from
the heart, rendering service with a
good will as to the Lord and not to
man, knowing that whatever good
anyone does, this he will receive back
from the Lord, whether he is a
bondservant or is free. (Ephesians 6:5-
8)

Yet, even knowing this truth we still find
ourselves facing the temptation to be a "man
pleaser" which, in turn, militates against being the
servant of Jesus. In fact, Paul makes it clear that
pleasing men as a core motivation and serving
Jesus are in direct competition with and
contradiction to each other. Consider Paul's
warning: For am I now seeking the approval of
man, or of God? Or am I trying to please man? If I
were still trying to please man, I would not be a
servant of Christ. (Galatians 1:10)

Do I want my boss to be pleased with my
work? Do I want my customers to be pleased with
my service? Do I want my employees to enjoy

working for me and for my company? The obvious answer is "Yes!" There is nothing inconsistent with following Christ and seeking to have those with and for whom I work to be satisfied and even thrilled with what I bring them. However, if I fall prey to the temptation to become a "man pleaser" at heart, at my core--if that is my prime motivation--then I have ceased to be Jesus' man in my business.

This temptation is not unique to business. Pastors often fall into doing what they do in order to gain the approval of their congregation or of some influential members. Missionaries, seminary professors, counselors all struggle with their motivation. So do doctors and teachers and politicians. Spouses make decisions deeply motivated in pleasing their partner.

Let's not sugar coat this and lower our estimation of the problem. This is not merely getting drunk with the boss because we didn't want to risk refusing or hiring someone who is unqualified for a job just because they are related to a co-worker. This is about our heart, our motives, our reason why we do what we do. And the heart, being deceitful and wicked (Jeremiah 17:9) is more than able to convince us we are right when we are terribly wrong.

I believe that there are three things that can help us face this subtle trap. The first two are fairly standard--time in the Word of God and prayer. Remember that "the word of God is living and active, sharper than any two-edged sword, piercing to the division of soul and of spirit, of joints and of marrow, and discerning the thoughts and intentions of the heart." (Hebrews 4:12) Time with God meditating on Scripture will be help keep your motives clear. Prayer, likewise, is a time for having God examine you just as David prayed, "Search me, O God, and know my heart! Try me and know my thoughts! And see if there be any grievous way in me, and lead me in the way everlasting!" (Psalm 139:23-24) The third remedy is accountability. Few believers live in any kind of accountability to anyone--to their church, to their spouse, to a small group. Even fewer establish this kind of "keep me honest" relationship regarding life in the business world. Get a few folks around you with whom you can be honest, who will ask you the hard questions, and who will both encourage and reprove you; this is a great gift!

Moral Failure

People in business are not any more prone to immorality than those in any other profession; they are also not any less. It happens. Close working relationships, shared stresses and shared victories and long hours are prime environments for men and women to cross a line from platonic to romantic relationships. Add travel to the mix or trouble at home and you have a dangerous situation. Add position or authority and things are truly dicey. Tragically, I have known many over the years in the pastorate and in business whose lives went off the rails for this reason.

Joseph faced this and prevailed. How did he gain the victory? He ran. He resisted until resistance alone wasn't enough and then he fled. It didn't save him from being falsely accused or unjustly imprisoned but it did save him from falling into sin and dishonoring God. Can I suggest that there are times when you need to simply leave a setting, excuse yourself, be elsewhere?

David, who didn't prevail, learned a terrible lesson and expressed it to us in the psalms. He wrote, "Against you, you only, have I sinned and done what is evil in your sight..." (Psalm 51:4a) To remind ourselves that moral failure is more than just upsetting a relationship or violating social or professional standards is powerful; to remember that it is offending our God and Master is a strong deterrent.

There are, of course, other types of immorality. Lying to clients. Padding expense reports. Embezzling. Fraud. Endangering employees. The list is practically endless. I believe that the things that help us escape the temptations of sexual impropriety are also sufficient for other snares. Keep in mind always that "no temptation has overtaken you that is not common to man. God is faithful, and he will not let you be tempted beyond your ability, but with the temptation he will also provide the way of escape, that you may be able to endure it." (1 Corinthians 10:13)

Hubris

Hubris means arrogance and self-importance. It is common in the business community and even considered a virtue by some--although Jim Collins did a good job of debunking the value of charisma and uber-self-confidence in Good to Great. Much of the self-help practices taught by well known "gurus" is based on the all importance of me and self-reliance is portrayed as one of the ultimate human strengths.

Sometimes hubris comes with position or promotion. Sometimes it comes with success and achievement. Sometimes with income and possessions. Regardless of what it comes with we know where it comes from: the pit!

I remember being in a leadership development consultation with a fairly successful rising star. As the CEO and I listened we were both stunned by how many times he used the words "I" or "me" compared to the relative non-use of "we" or "they." To listen to him tell the story he was pretty much singlehandedly responsible for every account sold, every order filled and every dollar generated.

Compare this with the guidance offered in Romans 12: "For by the grace given to me I say to everyone among you not to think of himself more highly than he ought to think, but to think with sober judgment..." (Romans 12:3) In other words, think accurately of yourself not expansively.

Self-Righteousness

Not far from pride and hubris is self-righteousness. The follower of Jesus living in the midst of pagans is always in danger of subtly beginning to consider himself or herself to be better than others.

Beware when you begin to define yourself by what you don't do. As the old rhyme goes: "I don't smoke or drink or chew...or go with those who do." I have often found myself in business meetings where another believer manages to let the crowd know that they don't do a certain thing. The implication, whether intended or not, is that, therefore, he is better than they.

Likewise, beware when you begin to define yourself by what you do. I go to church. I give to missions. I go on trips. I teach Sunday School. The incipient self-righteousness in this kind of thinking stinks and those around us smell it and want to gag and run the other way.

We would be wise to reflect often on Jesus' illustration of the Pharisee and the sinner:

> He also told this parable to some who trusted in themselves that they were righteous, and treated others with contempt: "Two men went up into the

temple to pray, one a Pharisee and the other a tax collector. 11 The Pharisee, standing by himself, prayed thus: 'God, I thank you that I am not like other men, extortioners, unjust, adulterers, or even like this tax collector. I fast twice a week; I give tithes of all that I get.' But the tax collector, standing far off, would not even lift up his eyes to heaven, but beat his breast, saying, 'God, be merciful to me, a sinner!' I tell you, this man went down to his house justified, rather than the other. For everyone who exalts himself will be humbled, but the one who humbles himself will be exalted." (Luke 18:9-14)

Political Attacks

If you are successful you will become a threat to small-minded, ambitious people. Count on it. Daniel certainly did (Daniel 6:1-9) and you will too. Politics and manipulation are a human thing. They are made up of half-truth, omitted truth, outright lies, intimidation, coercion, threats, self-serving promises--a pretty ugly list. Malicious politics have their source in Satan and often he attacks the faithful servants of God through their work in this way.

I remember recently I was preparing to speak at a BAM conference in Minneapolis and the week before the meeting I received an email from someone that was filled with such vitriol and falsehood that at first I thought it was a joke. Unfortunately it was not a joke but an explosion of anger, insecurity and accusation such as I have experienced only a few times in my life. It smelled like the devil and I am sure that is who inspired it. There wasn't a shred of truth in it. At first it upset me. I couldn't decide how to respond. Fight back? Expose the lies? I knew it was an attempt by the evil one to unbalance me before the conference, to derail what God wanted to accomplish by staging a threat on my position in the company. I prayed and also asked my wife (we call her God's Favorite) and my children to pray with me. As I waited on the Lord, a Proverb came to mind. Solomon wrote, "A soft answer turns away wrath, but a harsh word stirs up anger." (Proverbs 15:1) I chose that path and was able to see God sweep the situation away.

Many Christians are either naive about corporate politics or all too eager to engage in them. In my opinion we are not meant to be doormats but we are also not to live in the intrigues of the world either. Truth, integrity and a vibrant prayer life are the best ways to deal with these issues as they arise.

Loving Money

One of the most misquoted verses in all Scripture is 1 Timothy 6:10. People often say that "money is the root of all evil." This of course is untrue and a serious error. The verse says, "For the love of money is a root of all kinds of evils. It is through this craving that some have wandered away from the faith and pierced themselves with many pangs." (1 Timothy 6:10, italics mine) What is condemned is loving money and craving wealth.

Jesus spoke more about money and possessions than any other single topic. More than heaven or hell. More than salvation. More than love. Why? Because greed and lust and envy and covetousness are fundamental issues in every life. Children learn to snatch and say, "Mine!" People learn to resent what others have, to earn what others earn, to own what others own...plus a little more. It is the universal human competition to try to have more than the next guy. Much of business is built on this reality.

The Christian in business seeking to see God's kingdom come will certainly face the temptation of desiring to see his or her own kingdom established. Money too easily moves from being a tool to being a goal, a thing valuable in and of itself.

To be sure, this problem is not limited to the wealthy or prosperous. Some of the greediest lovers of money I have ever met were poor. Having is not the problem. Being had is. Possessions are not the issue; it's being possessed that we need to fear.

Two disciplines can aid the 2IC as he or she navigates the whitewater of business and wealth: generosity and heavenly mindedness. Nothing cures the love of money or holds it at the door than generous giving to those in need. I believe that one of the reasons that God instituted business in the creation is to generate wealth. I also believe that one of the reasons He enable us to generate wealth is to generously give it away. Heavenly mindedness means simply realizing that life here is short and eternity in heaven is long. As one friend of mine, a BAM practitioner in China, says, "The books don't close until eternity." We are not living for this world but for the glory of God. Don't waste your energy or your love on money.

Symbolism

I have gotten a lot of laughs at conferences and other speaking engagements by pointing out my pet peeve of fish logos on cars. I like to say, "We proclaim Jesus with our bumper stickers and drive like the devil." Serving the Son of God is a lot more serious than a decal or a trite phrase.

The obsession of Christians worldwide with symbolic, superficial insignia rather than spiritual power and love is tragic. Whether it's a cross around the neck or a Bible on the desk we seem to think that "showing" our faith is what God intended. Perhaps the most egregious example of this is something I saw in a Christian bookstore. Next to the check out counter was a package of "Testa-Mints"--little breath fresheners and candies with Scripture on them. Who thinks these things up? Who thinks they affect the world?

It is an easy and low risk thing in most

cultures to display our "Christianity" in some way. It is also something that means nothing to those around us. What the world needs to see is Jesus living in and through us in powerful, spiritual reality. They need to see love (John 13:34-35). They need to see compassion and humility and service. These things are undeniable and irrefutable. They speak!

Forgetting the Main Thing

I once heard someone say that "the main thing is to keep the main thing the main thing." I'm not sure where that phrase originated but I sure like it.

What is the main thing to Jesus' followers? What is the purpose of it all? The Great Commission is clear: we are to disciple all peoples and teach them to do what Jesus said. That's it. That's the main thing.

How easy it is in the rush of life--especially the lightning pace of business to lose sight of why we are there in the first place. We are there to provide a service. We are there to make and sell a product. We are there to find customers and to make money. All that is true. But the main reason we are there is to be a part of God's restoration of all things to Himself in Christ and to participate in the manifestation of His Kingdom and power and glory on this earth! Pure and simple.

I think we in business need to regularly take stock and examine ourselves to determine if we have lost sight of the goal, if we have been distracted or blown off course by all the shiny lights and squirrels of this world. We need a fresh does, a regular recalibration of old fashioned, Great Commission passion!

Conclusion

There are many other challenges and dangers that the "not the boss" Christian faces as he or she seeks to live out Christ in the marketplace. There are enough landmines and quagmires to fill an entire book much less a chapter.

These temptations are common to all people in all circumstances and not just business people. However, I do believe they are often magnified in business settings. Nevertheless, God is faithful. He has called you to business as He has called others to their vocations. He has located you where He wants you--at home or in a new land. And "faithful is He Who is calling you [to Himself] and utterly trustworthy, and He will also do it [fulfill His call by hallowing and keeping you]." (1 Thessalonians 5:24, Amplified Bible)

CHAPTER 15

THE PRACTICES AND DISCIPLINES OF THE KINGDOM PROFESSIONAL

As I mentioned in the introduction to this book one of the benefits of leaving my consulting business and going internal with a client was to experience first hand what God can do with the "not the boss," kingdom professional. I have been blessed to see kingdom impact in and through our company and I'd like to share with you some of the disciplines that contribute to this. The next chapter will deal specifically with real kingdom outcomes.

Intercession for People and the Company

When Daniel first heard of Nebuchadnezzar's dreams and threats to annihilate the wise men if they could not interpret it his first response was to gather his friends and pray. (Daniel 2:18). Jeremiah wrote a letter to the larger group of exiles in Babylon exhorting them to seek blessing where God had placed them. He wrote, "Seek the welfare of the city where I have sent you into exile, and pray to the LORD on its behalf, for in its welfare you will find your welfare." (Jeremiah 29:7) Jesus told us to pray even for enemies--much less our employers! (Matthew 5:44) and Paul exhorted Timothy "First of all, then, I urge that supplications, prayers, intercessions, and thanksgivings be made for all people, for kings and all who are in high positions, that we may lead a peaceful and quiet life, godly and dignified in every way." (1 Timothy 2:1-2)

About 10 years ago, while still consulting with my now-employer, I asked one of the leaders whom I knew to be a follower of Jesus to meet with me for prayer. For a decade now, he and I have been meeting over the phone every Monday morning at 7am to lift up our leadership team, our employees, our company and each other to God. We pray for salvation, for healing, for wisdom, for our investors, for personnel decisions and a host of other things as God leads. We have seen many answers to prayer and expect to see a great deal more in the future. The chapter on Kingdom Impact, I believe, is the direct result of these sessions with God.

What is exciting is to see how that has spread. In addition to Mike and I there are now many prayer groups, prayer teams and prayer meetings all over the company. We have been asked to pray publicly for meals, in thanksgiving, and for the sick--that is in public, business meetings! There is a group that meets consistently at every national company gathering in my hotel room specifically to pray.

Remember the words of Matthew Henry: When God intends great mercy...the first thing He does is set [His people] a-praying."

Openness Regarding Christ

In Acts 1, Jesus gives very clear and simple instructions to His disciples and, through them, to us. He said, "...and you will be my witnesses in Jerusalem and in all Judea and Samaria, and to the end of the earth." (Acts 1:8)

What is a witness? A witness is someone who tells what he knows. That's it. There is no requirement for great oratory skills or brilliance in apologetics. Nor is it necessary to have a sharp wit, outgoing personality, or a commanding knowledge of Scripture. It is only required that we share what we know. On this point there is no difference whether you are working in Kansas City or Khartoum. People need to hear about

Jesus. You know Jesus. So tell them what you know.

It might be worthwhile to remember that there are different types of witness. There is the obstreperous witness. Do you remember what this means? It means unnecessarily difficult. Don't be brash, condemning, a know it all, or self-righteous. That sort of witness never won anybody. There is also, and this is most common even on the mission field, the omitted witness. We simply don't do it. The time isn't right. My language is not developed. He doesn't want to listen. There are more than enough excuses to last a lifetime!

No, the witness we want is the gracious and opportunistic witness: "Walk in wisdom toward outsiders, making the best use of the time. Let your speech always be gracious, seasoned with salt, so that you may know how you ought to answer each person." (Colossians 4:5-6) Timing matters and God will provide opportunity. Manner matters and we need to be the conduits of grace and kindness when we share about Jesus.

My very specific recommendation is that every one of us think through our testimony. How did we come to Christ? What is different now? Write it down. Practice telling it. When you have the chance to share your story with an unbeliever in the workplace they are often surprisingly interested at the very least unable to argue with you!

A Model of the Way

Of course I mean that we should exemplify Christ and His truth in every aspect of our lives. People are watching you, observing your actions, your words, and even your facial expressions. Some are curious. Some are just waiting to see you mess up. Others, though, are genuinely interested and perhaps even impressed.

Here are some things to think about:

1. How do you speak about your wife or husband at work?
2. How do you treat your spouse in front of others?
3. What happens when you get angry?
4. Do you tell the truth?
5. Do you play politics?
6. Do you gossip or entertain it?

I don't want to create a new Law or some kind of 10 Commandments for Business. I only want to point out that it is in the very specifics, the mundane things of everyday life that speak.

Consider the very powerful impact of this kind of behavior on those with whom we labor:

> So if there is any encouragement in Christ, any comfort from love, any participation in the Spirit, any affection and sympathy, complete my joy by being of the same mind, having the same love, being in full accord and of one mind. Do nothing from selfish ambition or conceit, but in humility count others more significant than yourselves. Let each of you look not only to his own interests, but also to the interests of others. (Philippians 2:1-4)

> Do all things without grumbling or disputing, that you may be blameless and innocent, children of God without blemish in the midst of a crooked and twisted generation, among whom you

shine as lights in the world... (Philippians 2:14-16)

As you develop your walk with Christ and bring His grace into the office, warehouse or factory, there is a certain groundedness and centeredness that becomes apparent to those around you. Based on the research of James Kouzes and Barry Posner in The Leadership Challenge[3], this kind of internal gyroscope is what brings people to trust you. It is the context of trust, then, that your witness flourishes!

Development of Professional Excellence

It was said of Daniel that his work was excellent. (Daniel 6:1-4) Certainly gifts and divine blessing played a part in this. There is also, though, the human side of the equation. The side that says we must be ever learning and sharpening our saws so that we may bring more value to our employer.

There is a global temptation to assume that once I finish college my education is over. Or, once I land the job my development is done.

---

[3] James Kouzes and Barry Posner, The Leadership Challenge. Josey-Bass. 2003.

Especially among those of you who work for or will work for other believers in BAM companies I have observed an intellectual laziness and a professional lethargy that is shocking.

If Paul's admonition to do all things to the glory of God (1 Corinthians 10:31) is to be lived then we must commit ourselves to lifelong learning. Develop new skills. Learn another language. Take on a big challenge. Connect to another team. Attend another seminar. Read another book. I have no idea who said this first and it's been quoted by dozens; nevertheless it rings true. If you read an hour per week in your professional field you have a chance of staying current; if you read an hour a day you will soon become one of the experts in your area!

I want to be the very best in my job--from barista to board room. Otherwise I run the risk of my life, my professional performance tarnishing instead of garnishing the Word of Christ among men.

Availability to People

From my pastoral days I learned the hard lesson that people never need you on schedule.

Neither are they open to sharing their needs or willing to hear the gospel when it's convenient for you. They need you when they need you and they are open when they are open. Are you available?

Let me give a quick clarification and warning. I am not suggesting that you abandon your schedule or priorities at the whim of everyone with whom you work or interact. There are priorities and appropriate times. As the Preacher said, "For everything there is a season, and a time for every matter under heaven..." (Ecclesiastes 3:1) I am suggesting that we need to be flexible enough to embrace those non-scheduled, divine appointments that will come our way.

Notice, by way of example, Jesus and His interaction with the Samaritan woman at the well.

> So he came to a town of Samaria called Sychar, near the field that Jacob had given to his son Joseph. Jacob's well was there; so Jesus, wearied as he was from his journey, was sitting beside the well. It was about the sixth hour. A woman from Samaria came to draw water. Jesus said to her, "Give me a

drink." (For his disciples had gone away into the city to buy food.) The Samaritan woman said to him, "How is it that you, a Jew, ask for a drink from me, a woman of Samaria?" (For Jews have no dealings with Samaritans.) (John 4:5-9)

Here's the point. Jesus was tired yet He made time for someone else. Jesus was a Jew yet He reached out to a Samaritan. The rest of the story is a wonderful account of the conversion of an entire village. Imagine what might have been the outcome had Jesus simply said, "Make an appointment!"

Discernment of God's Spirit

God is always at work. Do we see it? Are we discerning? Can we see where God is working and in whom God is working?

I have a dear brother in Brazil named Gilberto who works for a large multinational bank. He used the phrase with me the last time I was with him that he wanted to "sow seed in fertile soil." I've not forgotten that. Where is the fertile soil? Whose heart is ready?

You may say, "That's not my responsibility." And from one perspective you would be right.

However, there is a discernment of the Holy Spirit for which we should pray. There is a divine perceptivity that we need. Consider this encounter between Peter and Simon the Sorcerer:

> Now when the apostles at Jerusalem heard that Samaria had received the word of God, they sent to them Peter and John, who came down and prayed for them that they might receive the Holy Spirit, for he had not yet fallen on any of them, but they had only been baptized in the name of the Lord Jesus. Then they laid their hands on them and they received the Holy Spirit. Now when Simon saw that the Spirit was given through the laying on of the apostles' hands, he offered them money, saying, "Give me this power also, so that anyone on whom I lay my hands may receive the Holy Spirit. "But Peter said to him, "May your silver perish with you, because you thought you could obtain the gift of God with money! You have neither part nor lot in this matter, for your heart is not right before God. Repent, therefore, of this wickedness of yours,

and pray to the Lord that, if possible, the intent of your heart may be forgiven you. For I see that you are in the gall of bitterness and in the bond of iniquity." And Simon answered, "Pray for me to the Lord, that nothing of what you have said may come upon me." (Acts 8:14-24, italics mine)

Peter perceived the issue of Simon's heart. In the same way, we need God's Spirit to inform our perceptions so that we can know where He is at work and what we are dealing with.

Walking in Humility and Love

There is no argument against love. There is no attack against humility that can prevail. "Therefore be imitators of God, as beloved children. And walk in love, as Christ loved us and gave himself up for us, a fragrant offering and sacrifice to God. (Ephesians 5:1)

I find it encouraging (to say the least) that recently two of my employees were having dinner with me and another team member (who is a passionate follower of Jesus). Without prompting, one blurted out with tears, "Will you please tell

me about your faith? I don't get it! I don't have it!"
She and the other employee listened with rapt
attention as the Christian team member and I
shared our testimonies and the gospel. I have
rarely seen love and humility open doors like this!

Conclusion

It would be easy to think that Joseph and
Daniel were effective just because of God's
blessing. It would be easy to think that because
folks back home are praying for you that God will
automatically work. But there is also my side of
the story. As Paul explained in 1 Corinthians, "I
worked harder than any of them, though it was
not I, but the grace of God that is with me." (1
Corinthians 15:10). There is a rest and abide side
of walking with God in business and there is also
a spiritual and practical discipline side. We need
to embrace both if we are going to see God work
in our work!

CHAPTER 16

KINGDOM IMPACT AND OUTCOMES

Nothing is more important in the minds of entrepreneurs, investors, leaders and their supporters than results. Process matters but outcomes trump all. Therefore, it is vitally important that we understand and agree on what kingdom impact and outcomes are...from God's perspective...in the realm of Business as Mission. These are especially meaningful to the 2IC and the "not the boss."

Defining Success

If we or those around us define meaningful impact in the traditional way, then we are limited to a small handful of areas. Every pastor and missionary understands this. BAM leaders and employees need to understand this as well. The first traditional definition is conversions. We are constantly asked, "How many people have come to Christ as a result of your ministry?" or "How many people have believed through your business in Boola Boola Land?" Having equated the Great Commission with soul winning it is not surprising that the Christian public wants to know the answer to this question. The second is church plants. Apart from any Scriptural mandate to plant churches we have come to describe modern mission and outreach activity in terms of church planting, congregations launched, sites activated. or remote satellite access locations. In fact, for the 21st century this is the metric everyone is focused on. A distant third is Bible studies started--in the community or in the factory. And way down the list is any type of social impact or social justice efforts such as orphan care, job creation or addressing human trafficking.

What is often at stake in these accepted metrics and definitions of kingdom impact and our relative ability to deliver or not deliver is financial support. Without tangible results that align with these expectations givers cool in their ardor and money goes elsewhere. The consequences of failure to deliver is to lose support and have to return home or go back to the congregation seeking increased giving--an activity far too many traditional pastors and missionaries spend far too much time doing.

BAM practitioners face less of this financial pressure (although some startups are donor funded and some investors think like ministry supporters) than professional ministry types. Nevertheless, we can fall victim to discouragement, misunderstanding, accusations of time wasting and so forth if we, like our professional ministerial brothers and sisters, continue to define success in the same old tradition way. Stated bluntly, at some point in your career in BAM you will begin asking yourself, "Where are the converts? Where are the churches? Where are the Bible studies?" If your answers to those questions is minimal then you will feel like a failure and, to make matters worse, your network of friends will gather around you as Job's counselors to pour on the guilt and condemnation.

I remember one brother who operated a kingdom company in Shanghai sharing his story with me. His witness was strong and the relationships he and his wife built with local Chinese were strong. However, when they came home for a rest and to see family their local church didn't know what to do with them. Were they missionaries? Business people? What "fruit" had they borne? It was an extremely frustrating and discouraging experience for my brother.

As long as we measure ourselves against the wrong standards we will either come out to be "successful" in what doesn't matter or we will beat ourselves senseless (and our friends will join in) for not delivering the "kingdom goods." Returning to our two great examples: Joseph was used by God to save two nations yet there is no evidence of any professions of saving faith or churches established; Daniel served as a trusted advisor to multiple empires but also lacked the accepted measures of success!

What we need is to rethink our definition of success, of what true kingdom impact looks like. The rest of this chapter will attempt to help us do just that. I base these words on both Scripture and my experience as a "second in command."

Conversions and Churches Established

"Now hold on, Mike," you protest. "Didn't you just say that these are not the metrics we need to use?" Actually, what I said was these are not the only metrics we need to consider. It is impossible to read the New Testament, especially the Gospels and the Acts of the Apostles, and not see the premium value God places on proclaiming the individual gospel and seeing men and women brought to saving faith in Jesus Christ. Luke's version of the Great Commission is entirely about preaching the Good News: "Thus it is written, that the Christ should suffer and on the third day rise from the dead, and that repentance and forgiveness of sins should be proclaimed in his name to all nations..." (Luke 24:46-7, italics mine) Mark is even more explicit: And he said to them, "Go into all the world and proclaim the gospel to the whole creation." (Mark 16:15, italics mine) Consider just one example of the disciples carrying out this command. After chronicling Peter's Pentecost sermon, Luke writes this:

> And with many other words he [Peter] bore witness and continued to exhort them, saying, "Save yourselves from this crooked generation." So those who received his word were baptized, and there were added that day about three thousand souls. (Acts 2:40-41)

And what do believers do? What do new converts do as when they come to know Jesus? They meet. They gather. They assemble. And that is a church. The word in Greek for "church" is ecclesia, which means "assembly."

And they devoted themselves to the apostles' teaching and the fellowship, to the breaking of bread and the prayers. And awe came upon every soul, and many wonders and signs were being done through the apostles. And all who believed were together and had all things in common. And they were selling their possessions and belongings and distributing the proceeds to all, as any had need. And day by day, attending the temple together and breaking bread in their homes, they received their food with glad and generous hearts, praising God and having favor with all the people. And the Lord added to their number day by day those who were being saved.   (Acts 2:42-47)

This is the New Testament pattern. The gospel is proclaimed. The Holy Spirit convicts and converts men to Christ through faith. The new believers begin to assemble. They begin "to church" as the Body is formed by the Spirit. In our company we have seen this on a number of occasions. It is a wonderful and glorious reality and one for which we should strive and pray as we live for Jesus in this world--in the church, on the mission field, on Main Street or in the village bazaar. It is not, however, the whole story!

Encouraged Believers

One of my favorite characters from Scripture is Barnabas. His very name means "Son of Encouragement" and that is just what he did. One new believer Barnabas encouraged was named Saul; we know how that story ended.

Whether you are a domestic BAMMER or working in an Indonesian company, you will likely be connected to believers in the workplace who lack the knowledge or the courage to truly live out their faith in the kinds of ways we've been studying. What a difference it makes when someone stands for Jesus in the right way. Others begin to come out of the woodwork, to find their voice, to embrace their calling.

This is one of the most profound things we have seen in the company that I work for. There have been conversions and other life changes. And there have been many believers who, heretofore, were working undercover. They were often serving in their churches and quietly parking their faith along with their car in the lot. Now, there are prayer teams all over the company, the faith is openly discussed, prayers are often said before meals and meetings, mission trips are celebrated and supported.

One person who I delight to remember is Judy. Judy was a believer when she first came to our team but a very distant one. Her life was crumbling along with her marriage. As she worked God worked. She began to get serious about Christ and His Word. Judy's marriage sadly fell apart but she later remarried an amazing Christian and together they are a brilliant light in their church, their company and the lives of many.

Successful Projects

You might have to stretch a bit for this one at first but remember this: there is no aspect of life over which Jesus is not Master and about which He does not care. If we understand and embrace that there is no sacred-secular dichotomy in God's Kingdom and that "the will of God...is good and acceptable and perfect" (Romans 12:2) regardless of category it falls in, then we can see that any number of things may in fact be Kingdom Impact.

In the 1980 Academy Award Picture of the Year, Chariots of Fire, there is a scene early on when Eric Liddell's father says, "Son, you can glorify God by the peeling of a spud." Paul's words certainly support this: "So, whether you eat or drink, or whatever you do, do all to the glory of God." (1 Corinthians 10:31)

A great sermon preached in the power of the Holy Spirit leads to Kingdom Outcomes. So does the successful translation of a book of the Bible into a tribal language. Agreed? Of course! Then how about the successful ocular implant that enables a deaf child to hear his mother's voice? How about a drug that cures River Blindness or Ebola? Or a pollution reducing technology for the power industry? Or the completion of a new office building? Or...you cannot draw a line can you? Any activity done for Jesus' sake down to a cup of cold water (Matthew 10:42) is a legitimate Kingdom Activity and can lead to legitimate Kingdom Results.

Joseph's excellence of innovation and Daniel's excellence of governmental work were both prime examples of true Kingdom Impact.

Employee Engagement

According to a recent Gallup[4] study, a staggering percentage of American workers are totally disengaged from their work and another staggering number are actively looking for another job. As I often tell audiences, if you don't love your job then quit--either quit not loving it or quit the job. For your own sake, don't stay in a job where your heart is disconnected.

I believe that one of the most exciting Kingdom Outcomes we can achieve, regardless of our corporate status, is an engaged workforce, a motivated team. Many years ago, the Chairman of the Board, who happened to be my boss, called me into his office to fuss at me because, as he put it, "Why does everyone want to transfer into your division?" I couldn't keep from laughing when I said, "The question you should be asking me why don't they want to stay in their current division?" We had built a solid team with a clear vision, shared values, deep concern for each other and our customers and we had fun! And it was true. People were lined up seeking a transfer in. I don't blame them.

People are looking for a cause to be a part of

and they are looking for leaders they can trust. The disciple of Jesus at work is ideally suited to build the former and be the latter.

Societal Impact (Better Life)

Our company employees over 102,000 people a week on temporary assignments. In many cases they are unskilled, entry level or trying to get back into the workforce for some reason or another. In the course of the year we will employ over 500,000 such workers for at least a week, many of whom go on to get full time jobs with our clients. We rally around a meaningful mantra: Getting Good Jobs for Good People. It gives meaning to our work every day.

There is more, though. We have discovered that every worker we come in contact with represents, on average, a family of 4. That means that we touch in some way approximately 2,000,000 people per week--men women and children and that we touch about a half million people each year.

The question we constantly ask is "What is the impact of that touch?" Is it filled with respect? Is it filled with appreciation? Are we fighting to get them a safe job, a job that suits them, a job with a future? Are we pushing to get better wages? Better treatment? Out of these questions we have formulated what we refer to as "Better Life." Our belief is that we can help each of our temporary employees and their families take a step or two toward a better, richer, fuller life.

Some of the stories we hear from our nearly 300 locations around the US include finding health care for someone who could not navigate the system, landing the perfect permanent job that resulted in getting custody of their children back, or securing additional skills training so that they become more employable. Sometimes it's just giving them a friendly place to stop--to have a cookie and a Coke and talk to someone who believes in them.

I believe that Better Life is one of the most Kingdom oriented programs I have seen in any company anywhere. In my view, it is a classic example of Kingdom Impact and Outcomes. It is certainly something of which I am very proud and proud that my company came up with it!

Conclusion

As long as we take a myopic view of what life in the Kingdom of God looks like we will see very limited Kingdom Outcomes. However, the moment we are reoriented to what God's reign really looks like as it is revealed in Scripture (instead of our evangelical traditions) we will be like Elisha's servant at Dothan. Our eyes will be opened to see all kinds of wonderful things God is doing in and through us and we will see them everywhere!

CHAPTER 17

WHERE DO WE GO FROM HERE?

Business as Mission is more than a historical anomaly or a creative way to do traditional missions. It is a movement of God that is actually a return to the faith of the early church. It is built on a solid Biblical and theological foundation centered on the integration of all things under the Lordship of Jesus Christ.

While we still need more entrepreneurs to join the movement and surrender their skills and passions to God's purposes we also need to see a generation of BAMMERS raised up to work in the businesses the entrepreneurs start. The lack of qualified BAM managers and employees is a major constraint on the growth and impact of BAM.

On another front, the home front, there is no better place to exhibit and communicated the grace of God than in the workplace. The opportunities to speak to unbelievers who have given up on church and who will never attend a service are everywhere.

A Confession

In my first book, Business as Mission, there is one point I made that I'd like to clarify and to a certain degree correct. What I was observing at the time within the BAM movement disturbed me. Business as Mission originated on the mission field and among the unreached; it represented a tremendous opportunity to get more players out of the stadium seats and on to the field. It was a grand opportunity. That is my personal passion. All of a sudden, it seemed to me, a focus on being a better witness in the domestic workplace began to emerge and in many ways distract those interested in going into business among the unreached. It was easier and certainly more comfortable to remain at home and be a good Christian at work. I confess I came down pretty hard on this. Too hard.

I still maintain that in the face of the huge need among the unreached people groups of this world and in light of the Great Commission, we need to focus our energies on getting outside of the church building and getting outside of our culture. We need to go where Jesus is not known or named. Specifically, I am talking about the

Muslims of North Africa, Central and SE Asia and the Middle East, the Hindus of India and Bangladesh, the Buddhists of Tibet and SE Asia, the atheists of China and on and on. It is virtually impossible to reach these people in the traditional ways. Business--real business led by real disciples--is the way.

However, I disrespected the call of God on those who stay when I wrote what I did. That was not my intention but, as I've learned in my life, intention isn't what matters. Impact matters. So, to those who felt "dissed" by my words, I apologize. The truth is that God is sovereign and His call on your life, His theography for you is what matters and nothing else.

A Balanced Approach

The truth is that 95% of the churches global resources operate outside of the areas of the world where 95% of the unreached live. That is compelling to me. And the truth is that God is Lord of the whole church in the whole world. That is compelling as well.

Business as Mission cannot be defined as only foreign. What does that word mean anymore in an increasingly small world? And if I go to Indonesia to do business for God is that business as mission? And in the process of serving in Indonesia if I equip an Indonesian brother to do business to the glory of God where he lives is that not business as mission?

Business in reached lands and business in unreached lands and business in least reached lands all have the same purpose--to see God's Kingdom come in the hearts and lives of men and to transform the societies in which they live to His honor and glory!

Four Outcomes

In Third Path we emphasize that we are equipping emerging leaders for full on participation in Business as Mission. With that in mind, we have identified four equally important outcomes that are entirely dependent upon what God calls the individual to do.

1. International Entrepreneur
2. International Employee/Manager
3. Domestic Entrepreneur
4. Domestic Employee/Manager

The purpose of this book has been to encourage the employee or manager whether overseas or at home. I hope this has been achieved.

Dare to Be a Daniel (or a Joseph)

Daniel and Joseph serve as great examples of those of us who work for others. They are examples that demonstrate that we are not a "lesser breed." We are not consigned to a subordinate role. We are in the place that God has sovereignly placed us and we can fully expect God to use us in that specific setting.

The lessons of their lives are lights to help us navigate the world of "2IC," Second in Command, employee and manager. Lift up your eyes. See the opportunity and seize it. Rejoice that God has a plan for you as much as He does for any other and that He has uniquely prepared you in character and skill to walk in that plan.

This is Business as Mission for the Rest of Us!

Printed in Great Britain
by Amazon.co.uk, Ltd.,
Marston Gate.